SEACOOK

SEACOOK

A GUIDE TO GOOD LIVING AFLOAT

Bob Heppel

ADLARD COLES LIMITED
8 Grafton Street, London W1

Adlard Coles Ltd
William Collins Sons & Co. Ltd
8 Grafton Street, London W1X 3LA

First published in Great Britain by
Adlard Coles Ltd 1978 (ISBN 0 229 11596 9)
Reissued in paperback 1986

Distributed in the United States of America
by Sheridan House, Inc.

British Library Cataloguing in Publication Data

Heppel, Bob
Seacook: a guide to good living afloat.
1. Cookery, Marine
I. Title
641.5'753 VC370

ISBN 0 229 11784 8

Printed and bound in Great Britain by
R. J. Acford Chichester Sussex

Dedicated to
MISTRESS SOFTLY
and those who cooked aboard.

ACKNOWLEDGEMENTS

First I would pay tribute to old Joe Edmunds, barge skipper, who in 1920 first fired my passion for cooking afloat by presenting the barge 'boy' with the whitest lightest dumplings which ever accompanied a beef stew, and all from an old iron pot on a tortoise stove while waiting for the tide in the Swin Channel.

All cooks are indebted to and share their experiences with the authors of books on cooking and wine. My indebtedness I here declare to my leading lights, who go with me wherever I sail. To Marie Comtesse, Guy de Toulouse-Lautrec, Mrs Beeton, Eliza Acton, Alice B Toklas, Elizabeth David, Jane Grigson, Mary Novak, Babs Honey, Robert Carrier, Robin Howe, Robin McDouall, John Doxat, L W Marrison and Cyril Ray I owe the delights I have tasted and such skill at the stove as I possess.

To one, alas now no more, a great restaurateur and genius with food, whom I was honoured to count as a friend, to Commendatore Peppino Leoni I would offer a vale.

No author could ever pay the debt to the one who read the manuscript, struggled with the calligraphy, corrected syntax, amended spelling, found missing paragraphs and presented typed order as a result. My debt is owed to Hilda Carey who did all those things, bless her.

Finally, to my *Mistress Softly*. She has carried me far in spite of my ineptitudes, fought wind and wave with me, kept me warm and dry and, safe in anchorage, lulled me to sleep. For all this the skipper is truly thankful.

CONTENTS

INTRODUCTION

Sailing, once the pastime of kings and a privileged few, has by the use of new materials and methods of production reached the multitude. Naval architects, designers and draughtsmen, mould makers, shipwrights, sales managers, advertising agents and a considerable proportion of the magazine press have devoted their energies to catering for the family man who, with his wife and children, wants to cruise in coastal waters. Expertise and considerable research have produced within such a family's financial reach, a stable hull, some auxiliary power, an efficient sail plan, room for sleeping, a space for storage, toilet facilities and some provision for cooking food. Functionally designed may well describe the small cabin cruiser's accommodation, its power unit, its fittings and running gear. Technological skill of a high order has given the sailing man – or woman for that matter – the means of ascertaining his direction, his speed through the water, the force and direction of the wind and the depth of the water over which he moves. He can predict the whereabouts of unseen coasts, have foreknowledge of the possibility of storm or calm, he can see with the radar's eye through the thickest fog and can call upon the wind itself to steer his craft. But if he calls upon his wife or crew for a hot meal he may well call in vain. For though research has covered his craft from truck to keel, from stem to stern and even reached the loo – it has largely missed the galley.

The galley of most small cruisers is a compromise borrowed from the caravan, was designed for a rectangular box and, installed in a curved space, only fits where it touches. In its most advanced form it can be summed up as two burners and a grill, with or without an oven, together with a sink. This summation does not make it clear that the stove top will not take a large saucepan and a normal sized frying pan at one and the same time; that the grill cannot accommodate anything deeper than a shallow pan in which a good chop will touch the burner; that to open the oven door and see into the oven one must lie under the cabin table and that the sink, which holds just a pint of water, cannot take crockery larger than a saucer. The results achieved with such equipment, combined with the ineptitude of an unwilling cook, are inedible, so meals must be taken ashore from quayside cafés, marina restaurants, in hotels, in ports, in coastal towns, in the rat race again.

The fundamental reason often advanced for the little attention given to galley design is the apparent lack of demand for good cooking facilities aboard. The oft reiterated statement from the wife, who joins her husband with the children for a holiday afloat, that she is not going to sea 'lashed to the kitchen sink' is quoted as proof. The woman aboard does not wish to become a galley slave. Of course the majority of wives who share the potential pleasures of family cruising complain. They complain about the repetition of the same old kitchen routine but under very restricted conditions. They complain, justifiably, about the same old domestic tasks whilst on holiday and without the efficient facilities of the land-based kitchen, about the same old culinary chores but without the tools to do them. The limitations of space and equipment, the lack of fresh food, fresh water and even fresh air in the galley, the perils of explosion, fire and scalds, the difficulties of cooking whilst in motion, are all causes of justifiable complaint. They are also powerful encouragements to eating ashore.

But dislike for the galley tasks is not solely a feminine trait. The all-pervading smell of cooking confined within a small space, the greasy half-warm washing-up water, the stained plastic table ware and burned frying pan are equally repulsive to the all male contingent. They will subsist on a bacon sandwich for breakfast, will consume beef hash for lunch, and, if compelled by passage making, will spoon down their gullets the contents of any three cans for an evening meal. Little wonder then that, at the earliest opportunity, a real meal will be eaten ashore as a relief from such a diet. As always the easiest remedy is to dodge the issue. But eating ashore is rapidly becoming a very expensive item in the holiday budget, particularly the family holiday account. It is scarcely necessary to point out that the crew, eating their main meal in one of the quayside restaurants common to all ports and coastal towns, are swallowing folding money with every mouthful.

Cooking afloat is an acquired skill, as essential as all the others with which the competent sailor is equipped. Like all the others it can be acquired by practice supported by reading and study. But while books on seamanship, on navigation, pilotage and ship maintenance are legion, books on cooking afloat are few indeed and most of that few are mere primers. There are twenty times as many books on knots alone as there are on good galley practice. There are courses on most of the arts and crafts of the sailor but these do not include culinary skills. Yet the skills in navigation, experience in seamanship, expertise in the intricacies of the internal combustion engine, and knowledge of the wizardry of electronics are rapidly devalued if the crew, exhausted by cold, damp, hunger and thirst, cannot be warmed and nourished. Their yachtmaster's certificates, both coastal and ocean, if burned would not boil an egg and in a list of priorities it is probably better to run out of wind, run out of fuel and perhaps even run aground, rather than run out of food and fresh water.

In the hope that some change may come to the general attitude of lassitude to cooking afloat, in the hope that more attention will be given to the design of an efficient galley for a good ship's cook, in the hope that the crew's ever-open maws will be more enjoyably filled, this book is written. It is not for those who regard a boat as merely a means of transport between one nautical parking lot and the next, with a restaurant guide as a pilot book, though it might well serve as a guide to the quality of the café's cooking. It is directed to the owners of cabin cruisers who, with their families, enjoy sailing, love still unspoiled anchorages and who go to sea to escape from the traffic, the telephone, the television and *The Times*. If then, you delight in the open sea, if you love small islands, if you prefer anchorages inaccessible by road, up creeks or in coves, if you want to get away from the crowd, you must eschew the cafés, the restaurants, stay off shore and eat afloat. Then if your cooking is as good as your navigation and your menus are the equal of your course plotting, you will find the eating as satisfying and as enjoyable as your landfall. You'll sleep soundly at night, as well.

Angels and devils on horseback

Open a can of smoked oysters. Pour off the oil into a frying pan and add an extra dessertspoonful of cooking oil to the pan. Stone some prunes, a simple task if they have been soaked, even simpler if they are purchased pre-soaked and stoned in package.

Stretch some rashers of streaky bacon with the back of a kitchen knife. Wrap each oyster and each prune in a strip of bacon, pinned with a cocktail stick. Fry quickly in hot oil. Serve to the crew, in the cockpit, accompanied with gin and bitters. Vegetables for the evening meal may be prepared simultaneously in the cockpit by the crew.

Part I

LIVING AFLOAT

Section I

THE COOK

The cook is the nucleus of the economy

There is but one answer to the problem of cooking and eating afloat. It all depends upon the cook, who is the nucleus around whom all meals aboard originate. Usually it is assumed that in all cases the cook will be a woman, since she is supposed to be qualified by nature for the chores of cooking, washing, caring for the children and nursing the sick. This last endowment is indeed paramount, a supreme virtue in any ship's cook, because some show resentment when they see the meal, upon which they have slaved, going over the side after but a brief sojourn in the stomach. But it should not be assumed that the first or only woman aboard is able to cook at sea. The qualities of character required in a good ship's cook are not sex linked.

Inured to the motion and unmoved by the claustrophobic effect of a small cabin, the cook should be capable from the galley of leading the crew to good eating, just as the skipper from the cockpit leads the crew to good sailing practice. Since there is safety in numbers, it should be understood by all that the menial tasks of galley work, the preparation of vegetables, the washing of dishes, the fetch and carry of provisions are best shared. Too many cooks cannot spoil ships' broth, and the cook's call for hands to prepare salad should be greeted with as enthusiastic a response as the skipper's call for hands to change sail, especially if the salad is rather more exciting than lettuce, with tomato and cucumber cut small. So a good cook should be able to gain that mutual co-operation which, in a boat, turns a number of individuals into a crew. It is noticeable that good cooks never want for an opportunity to sail, and a cruiser with a good cook never lacks crew members.

The attributes of character required in a paragon among cooks are good temper, a sense of organisation, foresight and inventiveness, attention to detail, courage and a cool head in the hot seat. Good temper comes first and foremost, for he or she is one of a group engaged upon a corporate activity which demands willingness and concentration at all times. Cooking, particularly under way, is fraught with occupational hazards which quickly strain the temper of the easily aroused. The cook who, enraged, flings the burnt hash out of the hatch will undoubtedly score on the skipper at the helm in the cockpit. Only good nature and resilience will arm the galley slave with a fail-safe mechanism, to accompany the more demonstrative emotional components of character. A sense of organisation will provide the materials required for meals at short notice in the face of ephemeral changes of weather and temperature which are the constant background to eating afloat. Foresight and inventiveness will readily deal with emergencies or unusual circumstances, like the skipper's sudden desire to entertain the Muslim captain of an Arab dhow or how to provide the owner's pregnant wife with an answer to her repeated requests for anchovies with everything. Most skippers are socially impulsive and can readily outdo the examples quoted. Attention to detail is an essential in all cooking activities. Quantities of ingredients, procedures in preparation, timing of cooking processes, correct temperatures during such stages, all require concentration upon details if the dishes, the menus, the meals are to be a success. Finally, courage plays a great part in all culinary operations. The great dishes of the world were the result of courageous trial on the part of their innovators. The gods only smile on cooks who, from the hot seat by the stove, worship with taste and aroma, and risk the burnt offering en route. It takes courage to be the first to taste what you have cooked. Even more courage is required to offer it as food to a hungry, healthy, physically strong crew. The galley is no place for weaklings.

The cook's responsibilities

The ship's cook's responsibilities far exceed the production of meals. The galley and all its equipment are his sole responsibility. When the skipper drops the corkscrew overboard it is the cook's responsibility to produce a replacement immediately, though he would be a fool to hand it over; wisdom suggests he should hand over the opened bottle. The provisioning of the boat, the stowage of food stocks, a running score of the stores of food, cooking fuel and fresh water, the wellbeing of the crew, their comfort in warmth and dried gear and first aid are all properly the cook's domain. He may well be called upon to assist at the last rites, for it is certain that he will be the only person aboard in possession of the adjunct to good cooking – a prayer book.

The exploration of new cruising areas, the excitement of new anchorages, new marks, new courses which enthuse the sailing fraternity have their counterpart in the galley. Here there are also voyages of discovery to be made by the cook into new local dishes, local ingredients, local specialties. The cook's challenge should always be 'You catch it and I'll cook it!' and from the successful answers will come some of the most memorable moments in holiday cruising. Freshly caught sea food is all that is needed to induce a good cook to show the real skill he possesses. This may be proved with the following recipe (see over):

A marinade of fresh sardines

It needs no cooking. First prepare one of the following marinades in the proportions indicated.

Either (1) 2 tablespoons olive oil
1 teaspoon lemon juice
½ teaspoon curry powder

or (2) 1 tablespoon dry sherry
1 tablespoon ketchup
1 teaspoon wine vinegar
a dash of tabasco sauce

or (3) 1 tablespoon white wine
1 tablespoon lemon juice
1 teaspoon tarragon

Sufficient marinade will be required just to immerse the fish. Take the fresh fish (sardines, pilchards or small herrings) and cut off heads and tails. Split the fish, clean them and remove the backbones. Arrange in a dish and pour over the marinade. Cover and leave for 3 hours or overnight. When the fish flesh appears opaque it is ready to be eaten.

Serve the fish as a savory on buttered toast or as a cockpit snack on crisp bread. They also make a delicious additive to a mixed vegetable and grapefruit salad.

Section 2

THE GALLEY EQUIPMENT

The stove

First and foremost among the inducements needed to encourage a good cook must come a good stove. Certain minimum requirements can be set out for any cooker used afloat. First the stove top should be large enough to take a quart-sized saucepan or a pressure cooker together with a normal-sized frying pan, at one and the same time. A top on which it is possible to heat a large kettle or a frying pan, but not both together is severely restricted. Remember always that, unlike the caravan, a boat is not surrounded by miles of terra firma upon which to light auxiliary fires or to set up extra burners for more pots and pans. There is the space of the galley and no more, for it has long been forbidden to walk on the water. Before you believe the stove to be large enough, therefore, arm yourself with a rectangle of card upon which your pressure cooker and frying pan fit; this is the pattern. Don't be distracted with suggestions that there are smaller pots and smaller pans. They do a smaller job – and who wants smaller meals when healthily sailing?

Ideally the stove should have at least two burners and a grill. The grill pan must be large enough to take four pork chops and the distance between chops and the burner must be sufficient to prevent the flames licking the chops before you do. To test for size take a large nautical almanac and put it beneath the grill in the pan. It may be felt that an oven is also a necessity. Roasting and baking are time-consuming processes, usually measured in hours, and time is at a premium while enjoyably sailing. With the exception of bread and pastry, most roasting dishes can be pot-roasted in the pressure cooker in a much shorter period. If, however, it is resolved to install an oven, make sure that the oven door may be opened and the inside examined without crouching in the loo or slipping a disc under the cabin table. Check the size of the oven, an adult shoe box is a good approximation. Envisage a chicken for four replacing the shoe box and do not allow your suspicion that the oven is too small to be lulled by suggestions that re-heated chicken pies are an alternative to a roasted bird. Reject the small oven. If asbestos mats are used on the top burners, a covered baking dish will enable the pies to be warmed. An oven is not then necessary.

The stove must have a fiddle rail around the four sides. These rails must not prevent the frying pan from sitting flat on the stove top. Some stove fiddle rails are so high that the projecting pan handle rests on the rail, thus preventing the pan from lying flat on the burner. A pair of adjustable locking bars should be fitted to the rails so that pots may be rigidly fixed; a substitute for such locking devices may be made from wire. If a ring is formed which will fit the exterior of the saucepan or pot, and from the ring a hook is contrived which will catch over the fiddle rail, the pot will be securely anchored.

Finally, as they say in the world of cooking afloat, 'to gimbal or not to gimbal'. Gimbals, that method of suspension which will enable the stove to remain horizontal no matter what angle the ship adopts, are essential to cooking afloat, and not only when cooking under way. For an exposed marina in a heavy blow can closely resemble the confused sea of a tide-way race. Gimbals will also preserve soup on calm days from the attacks of passing power boats, the wakes of inquisitive trippers or the unannounced jump of visitors on the deck above. A fully gimballed stove which can respond to pitch as well as to roll takes up a considerable space in a galley since the stove must be free of obstruction from bulkhead, hull or galley carcass in both directions. Some ocean sailing craft have solved the problem by installing two independently swung burners, gimballed in both directions, from which the separate pressurised fuel cylinders are attached to act as ballast. This solution loses both grill and oven. If there is not sufficient room for swing in both arcs, choose thwartship roll compensation first. Craft under sail list to leeward, and thwartship roll motion from wind and wave is more frequent than pitch. In some fast motor craft stoves are permanently fixed, since pitch is frequently more violent at speed. When the gimballed stove is installed, check that the centre of gravity of the largest cooking pot, when full and placed on the stove top, is below the pivot of the stove suspension. It is also necessary to fit a locking device which can immobilise the stove if required, so that cooking utensils cannot be upset by inadvertently leaning on the stove during preparation.

While considering the boat, the stove and the saucepans in motion, it is as well to envisage the cook in a similar situation. A snap ring fastening on a nearby strongpoint for the cook's safety harness, and two hand holds within easy reach from the stove, will help the cook under the most difficult conditions. Cooking so often requires two hands that the old adage of 'only one hand for the boat' does not apply in the galley. So gimbal the stove and suspend the cook.

The source of heat and stove installation

The choice of fuel for the cooker is a much debated and vexatious subject. Bottled pressurised butane or propane gas is the cleanest, most efficient, the most economical and most readily controlled source of heat on a small boat. The snag is its explosive nature when mixed with a sufficiency of air. One hears every year of boats damaged and crewmen injured by gas explosion. Probably an equal number of incidents caused by motor fuel or bad weather or just stupidity pass unnoticed in any sailing season. Such events are not so spectacular as explosion and therefore attract less publicity. But explosion can only arise from an uncontrolled escape of cooking-gas fuel. Once this potential source of danger is recognised, if the most elementary precautions are taken as an inflexible routine, then the chances of explosion are no greater than any other common result of carelessness, like striking a rock or sinking as a result of collision.

Precautions begin with a careful and correct installation. Butane and propane gas suppliers and stove manufacturers, as well as the nautical authorities and insurance companies, lay down safety standards for installation which must be followed strictly. If the pressurised gas cylinder is firmly secured in its own compartment (preferably on deck), separately vented to the air and draining over the side, remote from all electrics and as far as possible from the engine-fuel storage, then the prime source of danger is controlled. The piped supply should be as short as practicable, should consist of as few junctions and unions as possible and should be easily accessible throughout its whole length. The pipe used should be of seamless copper, in one run. Flexible metal hose and rubber tubing are less safe and require frequent inspection for renewal. The unions at the gas-cylinder valve and the stove should be sealed with the compound recommended by the manufacturers for such installations, and these should be checked regularly. This is rightly the cook's responsibility. Finally, and this must be an inflexible routine for every ship's cook and all who use the stove, *the gas must be turned off at the cylinder source after each period of use*, even though all the stove taps are off at the time. If this routine is invariably observed, then risk of explosion will be reduced to a permissible minimum. Such a rule should not pose any problem to the members of the crew. It is readily recognised that the echo sounder, electronic log, the D/F set, the radio telephone and the lights are all turned off when their use is completed. It should not be difficult to adopt the same attitude to the bottled gas cooking fuel. Of course, the situation of the cylinder storage, the chore of going out into the cockpit on a cold rainy night after a good meal or the cold trip from a warm bunk into a dew-soaked dawn to turn on the gas before the first brew of the day can be made, are discomforting obstacles to a practice which is only common sense, but without which all on board are at risk. So TURN OFF THE GAS should be the grace of every ship's cook. Three meals a day for a crew of four, with the occasional brew of coffee or tea, will consume approximately one and a half pounds weight of cooking gas per day. Pressurised bottled cooking-gas fuel is available in most sailing areas. It would be wise to ascertain the availability of supply before a protracted cruise, to carry a spare bottle, and to check the necessity for screw adaptors to adjust the ship's installed equipment to local supply cylinder threads.

Other sources of supply for heat for the cooking stove aboard are paraffin or kerosene, and methylated spirit or alcohol. Preferred by many as a safer fuel, available almost universally even in remote areas, there are many types of stove designed to burn these liquid fuels. The pressurised kerosene stove, which requires a preheating phase with alcohol or methylated spirit, is less readily controlled as a source of heat while cooking, and is susceptible during operation to draughts. It is also very smelly and dirty if not kept scrupulously clean, and it can in its preheating phase, create vexatious situations in which squirts of unburned fuel and clouds of soot envelop the interior of the boat. Should a kerosene stove be installed, a length of fine steel wire and a tooth brush will be needed. These will enable the cook to clean the burners and to start the process of lighting the stove all over again, if patience has been preserved, to which last a hungry crew do not always contribute. Consumption of paraffin fuel for three meals a day plus hot drinks for a crew of four will average some three pints per day, together with a pint of alcohol or spirit per week – and in the hands of the inept these can make a lot of soot.

An alternative liquid fuel for the stove is methyl alcohol. One of the safest forms of heat, it is not as effective as pressurised gas. It takes longer to cook food, for as a fuel it does not produce as much heat, and consumption for a crew of four can be as much as half a gallon a day, which may present a storage problem. There are two types of alcohol stove, in one the fuel is injected through the burners under pressure, in the other the fuel is gravity fed to the stove; both require a preheating phase. The alcohol stove is the least dangerous in the hands of the forgetful and disorganised, since a fuel fire can be extinguished with water and there is no danger of explosion except under extreme circumstances. The fuel tanks of both alcohol and kerosene stoves are usually an integral part of the cooker, and filling with fuel can present a problem in boisterous conditions.

Having chosen the stove, look to its installation in the galley, to its surroundings, its light and ventilation, its protection from draughts and its accessibility for cleaning. Light and ventilation are most important to the cook and to the other occupants at meal time. The persistence of last night's curry in the breakfast air is a poor beginning to a day's sail, and the warmth of the cabin from the cooker is only welcome if untainted with the odour of cabbage. A cowled ventilator or louvred extractor above the stove is not a luxury but a necessity. The susceptibility of fibreglass hulls to condensation and the fact that cooking is a prime source of water vapour, call for serious attention to ventilation in the galley.

Light, too, is of great importance to the cook. A warm cosy glow in the cabin is poor illumination for the preparation of a meal and chopped onion is easily contaminated with flesh and blood in a dim light. A single light behind the cook's head as he stands at the galley produces gloom in the cooking area from his shadow. Two sources of light above the galley, one on the left and the other to the right of the cook, will illuminate a shadow-free area for preparation and cooking, so that what goes into the pot will be clearly seen. The accessibility of the stove for cleaning is so often forgotten that it may be assumed that galley layout designers have never seen milk boil over or soup spill. There should be at least a four-inch space around the back and both sides of any stove. If the galley carcass is covered in the stove area with a heat-proof asbestos lining, this should be covered with a detachable aluminium facing. Asbestos sheet absorbs spilled liquids and splashed fat, and is difficult to clean. A metal covering is easily wiped down after each cooking period. The stale smell of many a galley comes from the fireproofing liner, which cannot be cleaned.

Safety measures and fire extinguishers

No matter what type of stove is fitted, a fire extinguisher must be within easy reach from the galley. It must not be fitted above the stove, for it should not be necessary to put the hand through the source of the fire to reach the extinguisher. There are three common types, the CO_2, the dry powder and the chemical gas extinguisher. The CO_2 extinguisher is very effective and can be recharged easily after use. It is, however, a bulky piece of equipment, is heavy to use and is very messy. The powder-type extinguisher is lighter, is very efficient and is simple to use; it is very messy, as well. Activated by a CO_2 cartridge it is possible to examine the contents regularly and to recharge the extinguisher. The extinguisher should be shaken fairly often to agitate the powder which tends to pack by sedimentation if left undisturbed for a long period. It is well to bear in mind that the extinguisher powder is lethal to the moving parts of machinery. If a powder extinguisher has been used, the engine compartment, engine and particularly air intakes should be vacuum cleaned before the engine is run. The gas-filled extinguishers are of three types. The carbon tetrachloride type is not suitable on a boat. The fumes are poisonous and in a confined space, such as a cabin, can be lethal. The others use BCF or Dupont FE 1301. These extinguishers are extremely efficient, act rapidly and extinguish any fire (except the white signal flare!). They have the advantage that, installed in various strategic positions, they can be remotely activated. Light and easy to use, clean in operation and non-toxic they are probably the best choice for cabin use. Crew should not remain for more than a few minutes in a confined space if the extinguisher has been used, as concentrations over 5 per cent can cause dizziness.

It is much less important to argue the respective merits of the various types than to ensure that the crew are versed in their use, and know the position of the extinguishers, even in the dark. With the co-operation of the local fire brigade, a practice with the fire extinguisher ashore could be a vital part of fitting out. Do not leave it until too late to familiarise those on board with the method of using the extinguishers. The fire may not be bright enough to read the instructions on the extinguisher when the emergency occurs.

The sink

The second item common to most galleys is the sink, though it is not essential; two plastic bowls used in the cockpit are just as effective and are considered by many sailing men to be superior since they do not require skin fittings. If sink there be then it must be a sink in size and not an enlarged soap dish. It should be of stainless steel and a water supply should be an integral part of the fitment. Size is of paramount importance. The sink must be large enough to take the tableware items commonly used at meals. The average dinner plate is 10½ in. in diameter. A sink only 8 in. across is an abomination. Above all the sink must be deep; deep enough to hold a gallon of water at least. Even when half full it should be possible to immerse cups and mugs so that the washing of crockery can be achieved even in a popple. It is possible to purchase the stainless steel type of basin used on inter-city railroad sleeping cars, which has an incurved rim. Under unstable conditions this retains the washing water. The capacity of the sink does not affect fresh water consumption since it is usual for sea water to be used for washing up, a fresh water rinse being sufficient. There is no satisfactory alternative material to stainless steel for the yacht's sink. The surface of all plastic materials, popular in caravans, will scratch, and beetroot, curry and pickled walnut will stain the surface. Those scourers which keep stainless steel bright and clean will ruin a plastic surface in no time.

Fresh water may be supplied to the basin by gravity feed or by hand or electric pump. Whatever the method it must be possible to put not only cups and glasses but also jugs and kettles under the spout of the tap or faucet. A short spout set back from the sink edge will deliver water to the sink or to a tooth mug but will not fill a jug or a pressure cooker. The ideal type is the rotatable tubular tap which can be swivelled to move over and beyond the basin and which will deliver water to the largest receptacle. Drainage will rapidly show any inefficiency by smell and failure to empty the sink. The shortest straightest line from sink vent to boat's skin is the only route. All bends, curves and kinks are potential traps causing blockage and its odoriferous accompaniment. Like all skin fittings the drain outlet must have a stop cock. When going to windward the involuntary supply of sea water on the sink-side tack does not improve sailing performance.

Fresh water supply on board

The supply of fresh water to the galley is of first importance both to the comfort of the crew and to good cooking aboard. The greatest drain upon this supply is the sink. This is true both literally and figuratively. The greatest waste comes from such simple operations as pumping water to rinse a glass or wash a lettuce under the tap. It is all so very quick and easy. Yet surrounded by water, even in port, one can still be short of fresh drinking water, particularly if cruising in strange areas. On some small cruisers the day's supply is drawn off into plastic containers so that consumption may be easily and visually measured. Other boats economise by using sea water for washing up and for cooking potatoes or shell fish. Sea water for this purpose should be drawn at least five miles from shore, and even five miles may mean little more than dilution of sewage in some areas. A fairly reliable guide to the cleanliness of the sea water can be obtained firstly from its clarity and secondly from the healthy growth of marine life on the tide's edge. Death and decay in animal and vegetable is the litmus guide to pollution of the sea.

If cruising in foreign parts it is wise at first to treat any fresh-water source with suspicion. Supplies from marina water-points are usually reliable, but any supply anywhere which does not come from a pressurised main should be viewed with caution, and water from open wells must be classified as instant dysentery. If at all uncertain as to purity, treat the water with sterilising tablets. If there are young children aboard it is wise before use to boil water used for drinking, as tender stomachs are easily upset.

On some boats the sink is reserved for the crew's personal toilet, plastic bowls being substituted for food preparation and dish washing. For much of the sailing season culinary activities can be performed in the cockpit as communal chores. The worst of the galley tasks, the washing up, is completed quickly and easily by the crew if a production line is formed in the cockpit. A bowl of hot sea water with a bowl of fresh water to rinse and a space to drain the crocks will spread the work. If at the conclusion of the washing process, the bowl of dirty sea water is emptied into the bowl of rinsing water, the fugitive tea spoon, which would otherwise have been poured over the side, will be discovered before it is too late. Such a piece of organised team work saves time and tea spoons.

The stove/sink unit as a working area

The sink and stove are generally incorporated into a galley frame or carcass. Too often the sink is situated immediately next to the stove, making it easy to splash from the sink into the frying pan contents or to burn oneself on a kettle when washing up in the sink. It is a great advantage if the stove and sink are separated by a worktop space, which will be increased during preparation of the meal by the cover lid of the stove and during serving by the lid of the sink. No disposition should be accepted where the cook needs to reach across the stove to use the sink. There are similar disadvantages and a waste of space where the cooker abuts on to the sink at right angles. The cooking stove and sink should either be in line or in parallel, with standing space between. Fire and water should be well apart, for the chances of burns on the hands or the more dangerous flare-up caused by water splashing into hot fat or frying oil are too great to risk. The finest arrangements incorporate cooker, refrigerator or ice-box and sink in line in that order. This provides the maximum working space and separation within one unit.

The placement of the galley unit within the hull is as difficult as any complicated jig-saw puzzle. Opposite the dinette on the starboard side is favoured by many, since it puts the cooking area close to the eating area around the table. A central table situation with seats either side shifts the galley away from the centre of the cabin, and a thwartship disposition results. Where the companionway is offset to one side of the cabin trunk, the stove/sink area immediately upon one's hand on entry is favoured by those who insist on maximum ventilation above the galley which the main hatch supplies. This location is also subject to draughts. Users of paraffin or spirit stoves note and beware.

Ventilation and light are as important above the sink as over the stove. The previously recommended two lights for the galley will solve the visibility problem at night. An opening port over the sink will admit daylight and will also allow steam from cooking and draining pots to escape, otherwise condensation rapidly forms on the hull interior.

Prawn Medals

1 tin peeled prawns
2 egg whites
1 tablespoon butter
1 tablespoon soya sauce
1 tablespoon cornflour
8 small rounds bread
2 tablespoons cooking oil

Chop prawns finely, mix with egg whites, butter, soya sauce and cornflour. Whisk vigorously. Cut bread into small rounds about 3 in. across. Shape prawn mix into small balls and put a ball of this mix on each round of bread. Press down firmly to form a medal. Fry in oil until golden brown, drain on a paper towel and serve with Southern Splash.

Mix in these proportions – 3 parts Southern Comfort whisky, 1 part dry vermouth, a dash of orange bitters. Top with tonic or soda water. Add cube of ice.

Galley chores go well with the eating!

Section 3

THE GALLEY TOOLS AND TABLEWARE

see Appendix A

The choice of culinary equipment

Around and in the galley carcass will be stored the pots, pans, tools and tableware of the ship's cook's trade. It must be remembered that they represent not only tools, but also volumes and shapes to be stowed. Equipment on any boat under power or sail must be held fast, for the world of the ship is one of almost constant motion. In a seaway and often at anchor any object which is not secured will travel and scatter. The chromium hooks and plastic racks which serve for display or as retainers on the kitchen wall, only form pivots on a boat. So, too, those clip-in spice racks, rubber suction holders for tea towels and plastic pegs for oven gloves, which may serve well on a caravan, have but a limited life and use on the frequently and instantly changing incline of the galley bulkhead, under way at sea. When choosing pots, pans, crockery, cutlery, mincers and strainers, look for the stowage problem each will create and select carefully the size, shape and number to take aboard. When a galley locker is opened, how often does a torrent of enamel and metal shower about the feet, and how often when reaching for the wooden spoon does a lurch of the boat leave spoon and hook together in the clutching hand? Give careful thought to the essential equipment for cooking afloat and even more careful consideration to its stowage. Considerable adjustment to an existing galley carcass can be achieved by the insertion of division sections in drawers and recessed shelving in lockers or by adroit use of shock-cord dividers. If you are so fortunate, buy the cooking tools first and design the cupboards and drawers to accommodate them afterwards.

Despite the apparent incongruity, the work of a cook in a small galley resembles the creative activity of a conductor of a piece of music, for the range, the scale of the composition and the occasion for which the performance is designed will determine the instruments used. So, too, in the galley. The only instruments required for the early morning minuet of fried bacon, mushrooms, grilled sausages, with toast and marmalade are a kitchen knife, a frying pan, a plate, knife and fork. On the other hand a full 'symphony' of four courses celebrating a safe arrival in a new cruising area may well call for a pressure cooker, three saucepans, a full range of tableware for four with the odd introductory 'obligato' on yolk separator and mandolin (the cook's not the minstrel's). To cook meals which will make the crew forget about eating ashore will require more exciting menus which in turn demand a wide range of pots, pans and tools. While considering the choice of equipment remember the sailing man's dictum from the days of square rigged ships – 'If it's brought aboard it must be stowed. If it can't be stowed it goes overboard.'

The tools of the kitchen trade

The minimum of working tools needed to produce basic meals is represented by a sharp kitchen knife of moderate size, a large wooden stirring spoon, a plastic pan slice, a tin opener and two asbestos mats for the stove. This is the initial kit for the galley. With it the cook will be able to present the crew with a simple diet of plain, unimaginative, nutritious items. The crew will survive and will enjoy eating ashore as often as possible.

Envisage the varied cooking operations which can be undertaken just on the limited facility of two rings and a grill, regard the common processes used in cooking and the everyday ingredients which are prepared for the usual meals. Upon the basis of these three considerations choose the kitchen tools. The one kitchen knife should be increased by the addition of a large chef's knife for major operations, particularly on fish and poultry, a small paring knife for cutting vegetables, dicing fruit, a knife with a serrated edge for cutting bread, rolls and cake and three vegetable peelers which, with the crew, will form a team to save time and vegetables. The initial stirring spoon, wooden to save the coatings on pots and pans, needs to be supplemented by a ladle for soups and stews, and a draining spoon, for fishing in the cooking liquids. The plastic pan slice may be regarded as expendable, for the heat of frying will wear it rapidly. Add a plain wooden spatula for turning food in the pan and the slice will last longer. A pair of cook's tongs is a boon for turning and lifting sausages, picking kidneys from the pan and capturing elusive hot items. As for tin openers, in a moving world where once dropped often means gone for ever, two are better than one and three are better still. The hand held type is preferable. Wall can openers still require two hands for operation and in addition, a static wall support; the galley bulkhead often resembles a wall in an earthquake so that co-ordination between opener and operator can be difficult.

Gash discipline

With the can openers in mind, the very necessary gash discipline aboard should be considered. It is obvious that garbage and particularly empty metal and plastic containers proliferate in the wakes of cruising boats. Plastic does not rot away, so empties *must* be put into a gash bag for disposal *ashore*. If the voyage is protracted, and at sea that means more than 48 hours, cans should be pierced at both ends, metal caps should be put into empty tins to be jettisoned in deep water beyond the reach of tidal fall.

If the empty bottles cannot be stored or the nature of the thirst needs to be concealed, sink the evidence. Bottles must never be thrown overboard unless filled with sea water to sink in the depths. Bathers' feet suffer dreadful cuts upon the razor-sharp edges of broken glass washed ashore.

The tide lines of coasts are marked by the constant advertisement both to the popularity of certain brands and the thoughtless, dirty, anti-social habits of their consumers. High water mark tends to become the Coca-Cola line and rock pools are filled with the record of a thirst for beer. Abandoning rubbish is not a new disease. The garbage heaps of ancient civilisations are the archaeologist's treasure houses. Advances in civilisation and standards of culture are recorded in the gash of the past. The present era produces more unperishable trivia than any preceding period, not perhaps the best record to leave for posterity. Plastic, whether sheet or package, should never, repeat never be thrown overboard. Reward for such thoughtless acts of sabotage should be severe. A period under water freeing the prop, or doubled up in the bilges in order to clear the circulating pump, or dismantling a plastic blocked loo pump are punishments fit for the crime. Pity it is that they are seldom meted out to the original culprits. Gash discipline afloat is a measure of good seamanship – and it starts with the cook.

The cooking utensils

Basically all that is required is a kettle, a pressure cooker, a non-stick frying pan and a milk saucepan. With these something to eat and drink may be prepared. Cooking, however, demands a little more. The kettle must be of large capacity, large enough to provide hot water for a personal wash, a large wash up or a coffee party. It should be a whistling kettle, with one hole for filling and pouring. The snap closure of the whistle will prevent spillage when the kettle is full and the whistle will tell the cook, the crew and all adjacent craft that the water is boiling. This saves fuel, and it can save kettles which have been known to boil dry unnoticed.

Cooking requires more than just boiling water, and the cooking pot bears most of the brunt of the process. Bearing in mind the peculiar circumstances embraced in the single word 'afloat' – the limitations of space on the stove, and the motions of both boat and cook – it is obvious that the large cooking pot must be a pressure cooker. While James Watt was idly watching a kettle boil and discovering the steam engine, he could, had he been a hungry cook, have invented the pressure cooker at the same time. The principle on which pressure cooking is based is the harnessing of steam in a pressure-tight container, which would escape from an open cooking vessel. In the sealed container, the temperature rises above the normal boiling point of water and steam is continuously forced into and through the food to tenderise and cook it quickly. Pressure is controlled by a valve usually set at 15 lb. per sq. in., which also acts as a safety measure.

First and foremost the cooker has a locking lid. The pot when closed can be rolled, rocked and even dropped, but the contents do not spill. It usually embodies three additional compartments which enable four items to be cooked separately and simultaneously. Its greatest virtue is its capacity to convert the toughest ingredients into the tenderest tasty textures. It deals equally well with fish, fowl or meat, cooks vegetables to perfection, retains flavours and, above all else, cooks quickly. The pressure cooker saves cooking time, cooking fuel and the cook's time. There are a number of types, and complete directions for their use and some useful recipes can be obtained from the manufacturers. For good cooking on board the pressure cooker is a must, and a good cook deserves two, one set aside to preserve stews and braises, which may be kept for some days if brought to pressure every 24 hours and left sealed to cool.

Of saucepans for the galley, the best type are triangular in cross section, sold in sets of three, with lids. The three saucepans fit together to cover one burner of the stove. Thus the combination of three saucepans and one pressure cooker with three internal compartments will enable seven items to be cooked simultaneously on a two-burner stove. The set of three saucepans has a detachable handle which fits each in turn. This is a great space-saving device on a small stove top. The handle should be wiped after use and put away safely. It should not be entrusted to the dish-washing brigade for, once lost, replacement is difficult, and the saucepans cannot be lifted safely and easily without the handle.

The frying pan should be fitted with a lid. This prevents fat and grease spattering the galley surroundings whilst frying takes place. There are also a number of poached dishes which can only be cooked in the pan with a lid. Frying pans for boat stoves always present a problem, for most pans have a low profile and a long handle which must project across the stove top to avoid the fiddle rails. The second burner is then obstructed. There are frying pans with folding wire handles, which fold most unexpectedly. There are also small pans with shorter handles, too small for the crew's bacon in one fry. It is time that frying pans with detachable handles were designed and manufactured. But then it's probably more difficult than the designing of a self-steering gear!

As a luxury for the expert in the galley, invest in a deep fry. This has a number of uses other than producing fish and chips. But first a warning about deep frying generally. Frying in hot deep oil is an operation requiring a firm steady base. Rarely can this be guaranteed afloat. Even in the marina the unexpected passage by crew members of outlying craft across the fore deck can tip the ship irregularly and suddenly. This results in scalding fat tipped upon the cook's canvas-shod feet, an excruciating and dangerous injury. If fish and chips are to be deep fried, cook only a few at a time in shallow oil, keep the lid on the fryer, lock the pan on the fiddle and stand well back. Oilskin trousers and seaboots should be worn. The deep fry is better used to cook shellfish, cockles, mussels, whelks, to fry scallops and clams, to boil crayfish and lobsters. The basket lining of the fryer also makes an efficient sieve for washing lettuce.

The more specialised kitchen equipment

The galley equipment must include some kitchen tools which are specialised rather than of general use. Argument for their inclusion will range from the frequency of their use to their stowage problem. All can, however, add variety to the dishes served aboard. High on the list comes a knife sharpener. A knife is blunted by use and is a maddening tool for a cook faced with a 7 lb. dorado, freshly caught. There are knife sharpeners little larger than a matchbox in size which are well worth their place aboard.

It is rare for any main ingredient for a dish to arrive in a form ready for the pot. Knives, of course, are used to prepare the dish but three tools will change the size, texture and nature of food materials. They are the mincer, the grater and the whisk. The mincer will not only mince steak for breakfast but will also squeeze the juice from citrus fruit and pineapple, make breadcrumbs from toast and even coarse grind coffee beans, so it cannot really be considered a luxury; it is, however, somewhat difficult to stow. The cutter blades must be tied to the assembly for storage and the awkward shape is better boxed when put away.

Graters contribute to the savory starters and to the final appearance of many dishes. The half-round section of the common grater creates stowage problems, so search for the flat, folded type, a much better buy.

A whisk has a vital place in the preparation of egg dishes, not so much for the omelette, which may be beaten with a fork, but for pancakes and those mouth watering delicacies which are made with firm whisked egg whites. The rotary whisk is an excellent tool, but like the mincer also presents a stowage problem. The wire hand whisk is easier to stow but hard on the wrist when in use.

If pressurised gas is used as fuel for cooking, a gas lighter of the battery operated spark type is necessary. Matches will always be available, sealed in waterproof plastic containers, but matches should not be used to light butane or propane gas cookers. All too often the gas is turned on, the match is struck but fails to light after two attempts. A third match breaks in striking so the fourth match, now well alight, is placed at the burner. The result is a flash of flame from hand to eyebrows. Left turned on, the inflammable vapour, which is heavier than air, collects in the trough of the stove top just as would a liquid, and mixed with air explodes into flame the moment the match is applied. Remember this cautionary tale and don't use matches with butane stoves, use a spark lighter. Secondly, don't turn on the gas until the lighter is at the burner. If the gas does not light immediately, turn it off, wait a minute or two and begin the process again, putting a lighter to the burner before turning on the fuel. A battery operated lighter will save burned fingers, save matches and will not be lost, for it will not light cigarettes or pipes.

Tableware and cutlery

The minimum tableware for a crew of four is:

4 large plates
4 small plates
4 bowls (soup or dessert)
4 mugs

Plastic tableware deteriorates with use and washing, the surface discolours and stains. Tea and coffee stains may be temporarily removed with a solution of borax or with a metal pan scourer. The specialised crew ware designed for boats in plastic does not appeal to some. The 'crew plate' is trough like and will not hold cornflakes above Force 2, the 'crew mug' is too large for tea and too small for soup. Anyway, eating is the same process either ashore or afloat and pleasantly designed tableware looks as attractive in the cabin as it does at home. Just feeding is a different kettle of fish and in the cockpit is a hand to mouth process with paper serviettes, paper napkins and large hand-warming mugs.

As a material oven-proof glass tableware is preferable. It is tough, its surface does not scratch and it will not stain. It comes in a large variety of functionally designed shapes, of many sizes and in attractive colourful designs. To the basic requirements above should be added four breakfast cups and saucers, four egg cups and two large bowls. The bowls should be large enough to hold cooked vegetables, fresh fruit, salad or trifle. They should also be large enough to serve as mixing bowls for meal preparation. Two jugs will be needed, one measuring-type of one pint size and a large quart-sized plastic jug, with lid, for cool fruit drinks, ice and general pouring purposes.

The choice of glasses for drinks is best decided on two counts, vulnerability and appearance. Glasses of normal type are fragile, plastic 'glasses' are less likely to break, the material is softer and the designs lack distinction in appearance. Champagne in a plastic 'glass' always tastes like poor cider! So that they do not topple easily, glasses should be broad based and without stems, one of the best type is the heavy based small-sized tumbler type of glass, which is fairly durable, sparkles when clean and which doesn't warm up quickly when held in the hand (as does plastic). Stemmed glasses are usually fragile and relatively costly. Category MNO applies (money no object!). As to the number of glasses required, this depends, not upon crew number, but on the sociability index of the boat. Work out the multiplication and order accordingly.

The essential table cutlery for a crew of four will be:

4 knives
4 forks
4 spoons
8 teaspoons (4 will be lost)

The cutlery should all be of stainless steel. Avoid wooden or plastic handles for they will not survive the wear and tear, the hot sea water and the ruthless use for purposes other than eating. The large knives should have a serrated edge, not for tough meat because pressure cookery will never serve tough meat, but for cutting bread, rolls, toast and the like. One dessert spoon per man will suffice for it is difficult to differentiate between the action of spooning soup or spooning dessert, either may be blown upon to cool the contents and there is usually time to wash the spoons between the soup and dessert courses. However, two spoons per man get the galley an extra star in the cruising gazetteer and will be useful on social occasions. Teaspoons are needed in quantity because other than chaining them to the table, there seems to be no way of preventing loss.

The 'brew up' gear

The advent of tea bags and instant coffee has made the teapot and coffee pot out of date. The ritual of tea making as a social ceremony of artistic merit has faded with the departure of the social call for afternoon tea. For many, however, there is still no substitute for the early morning brew of tea and the forenoon mug of hot coffee. A tea pot for a cruising family or crew should be large, of enamelled metal, with a firm handle and a chain-attached lid. It should be possible to put the pot on the stove to keep the tea warm for a second cup, and it should not be possible to empty the lid over the side with the tea-leaves. The coffee pot comes in a number of forms differing according to the method used for making the brew. A large enamelled metal pot with drained lid and firm handle is the favourite with those who make their coffee with ground beans boiled in water. In the hands of the experts this method can produce the finest coffee to drink in the world. Some devotees add a tablespoon of cold water to the brewed pot to settle the grounds, others pour through strainers (add to equipment list). The essential features from the functional aspect lie in a robust construction which may be stood on the stove to brew for extra fillings, and a secure lid which cannot follow the grounds into the depths alongside.

Other afficionados extol the percolator. The two part, screw-thread joined pot with its enclosed filter, is rarely large enough if coffee is needed in mug-sized proportions. A one-pint size is readily available, larger percolators are rare. The glass percolator of quart size is large enough but rarely survives the first real blow, in both senses. The result of filtering the brew is coffee of another kind, ambrosia to some, dish wash to others.

Tea bags and instant coffee are very easily stowed . . . without the pots.

The total galley pieces as a stowage problem

The galley equipment once put aboard must be stowed. The root problem of storage lies in the galley carcass design. There should be at least two drawers and three lockers to every galley. One drawer should be compartmented into three sections for cutlery, the other should be partitioned for the larger kitchen tools. One of the lockers should be large enough and of special design for the storage of pots and pans. It should not be necessary to stow anything other than galley equipment in these drawers and lockers. All drawers aboard must have drop locks, while locker doors should be more secure than just clip retained. The compartments of the cutlery drawer should separate tableware from small kitchen tools, knives, scissors, skewers, tongs, tea strainer and measures. The second drawer should be partitioned for the larger spoons, ladles, slice, spatula and whisk, and it should separate these from the smaller, shorter equipment, the egg-white separator, measuring spoons and balance (there is a simple balance in metal, designed on the steel yard principle, with a sliding pivot, scaled to four ounces, which occupies less space than a ladle and pays for its presence every day).

The most effective stowage for pots and pans is in a locker fitted with a low shelf in which holes to fit pans, pressure cooker and pots have been cut. Ease of access for the large cooker requires a wide opening door. Saucepans stowed one inside the other and the lot piled into the frying pan create the situation in which it is necessary to remove all in order to reach the middle-sized pan. The disturbance caused by the clatter of pans and lids destroys the peace and quiet of early morning. This initial step in the preparation of breakfast, a torrent of metal on the cabin sole, rudely awakens the crew who, like Pavlov's dog, begin salivating. Soon an impatient line of gannets will be champing at the elbow of the cook, so sacrifice a deal of extras for a fitted pot-and-pan locker. Another locker in the galley carcass will hold the larger items of tableware, the bowls and jugs. It will also provide stowage for kitchen items of size, the colander, mincer, salad sieve (a collapsable type occupying no more space than a plate) the tea pot and coffee pot. The third locker is used for the season's bulk stores in labelled large plastic containers, the teabags, instant coffee, cooking oil, dried milk powder, sugar and rice; these containers should be clearly labelled, have well-fitting lids and be stowed in cut-outs like glasses.

Foodstuffs in quantity always create a storage puzzle. Those which can be repacked should be put into large plastic screw-topped rectangular containers. Circular sectioned packages waste a great deal of space. All repackaged items must be labelled. Ingredients preserved in liquid in glass jars or bottles should be wrapped in foam rubber sheeting fastened with cellotape, and packed close together inside a plastic box – don't allow cardboard boxes to be used for storage, they are too easily torn and are evidence of untidy makeshift stowage. The tableware should be racked in a separate unit, tailored to fit the crockery and near to the galley. It is well to line the crockery locker with foam rubber sheet. This will silence the plates and saucers as the boat beats to windward. Efficient tailored tableware stowage is an insurance against replacement and, if sailing any distance and at night, is an aid to sleep for the watch below.

Cleaning equipment and materials

These, the last of the galley gear, are the adjuncts to the kitchen sink to which the poor cook is supposed to be chained. Most are concerned with washing and cleaning. Detergent liquid, cheaper bought in bulk, soap powder for laundry work, polishing pads of steel wool, and scouring powder, are essential stores for the galley if all is to stay clean and bright. Stove, worktop and sink should be cleaned after each meal, as a regular practice. The galley, treated thus, will still look new after four years of wear. Left for four days, the cleaning neglected and spillage burned on to stained surfaces, and it will never be the same again. For cabin sole washing, brushes are preferable to mops or sponges. The seat at the dinette downwind of a stale smelly dish mop is not a place of honour. Nylon brushes are better and less smelly cleansers. A plastic box securely fastened to the galley bulkhead should hold the current ration of cleansing stores close to the cook's hand.

The cook's personal gear

There are items in the galley which the maître de cuisine may rightfully call his own personal possessions. The chef's armour, a pair of oven gloves, and a large bibbed and pocketed apron are the first line of defence against burns and scalds. No good cook anywhere goes into battle without putting on his armour. Even in heavy weather the apron should be worn over heavy woollies and oilskin trousers. It is easy to slip out of an apron down which scalding liquid has spilled, it takes longer to get out of a steaming hot pair of trousers. The cook's apron takes the brunt of the battle and after a good boil comes up smiling afresh. In the pocket of the apron, with the oven gloves, will be two corkscrews, two bottle openers and a box of matches, the kind which will strike anywhere. The close guardianship of these essentials is the cook's own responsibility and the items must never be loaned to anybody, not even to the girl on the quayside. For no booze, no beer and no baccy is more than a cook can stand and often in one or all of these lies the cook's only refuge.

Section 4

PROVISIONING THE BOAT

The importance of planning

The cook is responsible for provisioning the boat for the day, for the race, for a long week-end, for a holiday cruise or for the season's sailing. Though too many cooks cannot spoil the ship's broth, too many voices and choices can wreck any provisioning scheme. The cook with the skipper should form the executive committee, esecially if the skipper pays the bills. The determinants of stores for the planned programme are in essential, the number of mouths times the number of meals per day times the number of days afloat. Unfortunately, stocking up with food is neither a simple matter of arithmetic nor of the haphazard purchase of a selection of canned goods to be dumped in the bilges. Such a nonchalant approach leads after only 18 hours aboard to a menu consisting of kippers, saurkraut and creamed rice. Ships' cooks have been keel-hauled for less. A clear-cut programme of items and quantities for a known period of time, providing ingredients from which a permutation of menus may be devised, is the basis upon which the cook must work. It is also necessary to have an accurate assessment of the stowage capacity available for provender. What has to be left behind cannot be cooked at sea.

Provisions as perishable and preserved items

Forethought and preparation preceding the passage of food from plate to mouth are as important as the preparation for the passage of the ship from point of departure to anchorage at the voyage end. Much of the difficulty of this scheming lies in preservation, for fresh food is always a limited commodity in this yacht's galley whilst cruising. The refrigerator, taken for granted ashore, is at a premium aboard, and of this more later. But no refrigerator or ice-box installed in a 27-ft. boat could have a capacity for keeping a sufficient quantity of perishable food fresh for a crew of four over more than 2 or 3 days, and even a shorter period in hot climes. Fortunately the below waterline temperature of a plastic-hulled cruiser in most coastal waters, outside the tropics in high summer, will be cool enough to keep semi-perishable foodstuffs like cheese, longlife milk, longlife cream and smoked sausage fresh for weeks rather than days.

Preservation methods

The major part of all food material used afloat must be preserved, but this does not necessarily mean tinned or canned. Eggs may be preserved by coating them with Vaseline or petroleum jelly, wrapping them individually in tissue paper and packing them in dated egg boxes. Stored in the bilges, they will stay fresh for weeks. Eggs can also be pickled in vinegar, as can herring fillets, cucumber, onions and beetroot. Beef and green vegetables may be preserved in brine. Fruit may be purchased dried, vegetables may be bought in dehydrated form and both are much more easily stored in plastic packets, a great economy in weight compared to cans or jars and a very substantial saving in storage space. Brine and oil preserve sea-food items, shrimps and cockles, mussels and tuna fish for very long periods. Smoking not only keeps meat and fish but adds considerably to their taste. But for all this, it will be mainly canned goods which make up the greater part of the preserved food for the ship.

The stores list

Preparation begins by listing the food items used on almost every occasion, the dry goods, the constant constituents of the daily breakfasts, lunches and evening meals and the snacks. Whether day sailing or holiday cruising, whether passage racing or on a long week-end, this first section will include tea, coffee, cocoa, sugar, flour, rice, marmalade, cooking oil, breakfast cereals, etc. When day sailing, the perishable foodstuffs milk, butter, bread, fresh meat, fresh fruit, etc. will be added to complete the stores for such a short period.

A second list will deal with the items which must be added to the first if the sailing period is to be longer, say several days. This will need to include longlife milk, crispbread, french toasts, canned butter, meat and fish. For an extended cruising holiday over a long period and as back-up supplies for the whole season, a third list will be made. It will include a larger selection of canned meat, fish, vegetables and fruit, and composite meals such as curried chicken or spaghetti bolognese. It will include soup powders, meat-extract cubes, dessert mixes, the herbs, spices, flavourings and condiments and the long-term bulk stores for the kitchen sink.

The three lists combined will record all the items needed over the season. The quantities of each required will depend upon the sailing schedule and the number in the crew. A full suggested list is provided in Appendix B.

When the purchases are completed, record these items with the quantities beside each. This list will provide a total picture of the food supplies, and if the quantities are amended after each period of use, the list will show at any time the current state of the ship's stores. It is an advantage to have a duplicate list which may be carried ashore after each period afloat. It will provide a memo for the shopping required before the next sail and, if recent purchases are added, the list will be kept up to date. This preparation may seem laborious but winter is long and time spent on stores then will be time saved and anxieties eased when spring brings fitting out again.

The stowage record

The listed stores on the purchase record represent not only a quantity of food but also a volume and weight to be stowed. When the whole is assembled on the floor at home in the early part of the year the real headache begins. All has to be packed away into the variously curved spaces in the boat so that, spaced over the hull, the weight is distributed evenly, individual items will be readily available and each may be easily located at any time.

The plan of the boat is the guide to the disposition of stores, and the fitting of square pegs into round holes is a simple matter compared to the stowage of food on board a small cruiser. Weight disposition is important. Of course all the heavies in the stores are not stowed forward. The skipper's advice will be of a great value in this since he, best of all, knows the ship's balance and trim. The weight to volume ratio, too, presents a problem in the best use of large and small lockers. Quantities of breakfast cereal or dehydrated meals weigh little but in volume require large spaces. The glass reinforced plastic hull usually has good stowage, for bilges in such craft rarely run with water and one can stow below the cabin sole safely. Considerations of availability also have to be borne in mind. Are pickled onions needed at every meal, or is the salt only required once a week? If at the end of the stowage programme, the demand for an item at meal time requires that everyone leave their seats, revise the plan and begin again. So, with the boat plan and stores list to hand, put ready availability and priority of usage together and choose lockers accordingly. Lockers quickly accessible will hold those items used most frequently. Lockers below frequently used seats, e.g. the navigator's, should be used to store large stocks of bulk purchases, which are only drawn on occasionally for replenishment of the in-use store. Preserved eggs, cheese, longlife milk and cream, and tinned butter are best stowed in lockers below the water line. As these problems of stowage are examined, the advantages of lightweight rectangular plastic containers become more and more apparent.

Take the provision list, mark it off in categories and indicate beside each its location when stowed. When so planned it should be possible to locate the constituents of any menu with the minimum of disturbance. Replenishment quantities are always stowed according to this plan throughout the season. This location sheet could resemble Appendix C.

Marking the stores

When the season begins and the planned provisioning is underway, mark the stores clearly to indicate the contents of cans, containers and plastic boxes. Looking into a locker from above, all tins circular in cross section resemble each other, all square section plastic containers seem identical. Mark such containers and packets clearly on top with black felt-tip markers in a readily recognisable abbreviated code (John Illingworth's *Hentit* for Breast of Chicken is an oft-quoted ingenious example); lipstick also makes a clear waterproof mark on any surface. The saving of time and frustration from this orderly approach is considerable. The bad temper arising from a fruitless search for small yet essential ingredients, like meat-essence cubes, can reduce the cook, by nature a temperamental individual, to a raving maniac. When one considers how carefully sheets are coiled, tools are readily located, instruments and charts are racked and even a palm and needle can come immediately to hand, it seems odd that food lockers have been found to contain tins of jam, bottles of tomato sauce, an empty gin bottle, a left seaboot, a broken sail batten and an out-of-date tidal almanac. Such a conglomeration can only be a prophecy of the standard of galley practice on board. But when a cook sits back dizzy and aching from packing cans into holes, if the job is well done and the records are straight, at least the season has got off to a good start and it is unlikely that the crew will starve.

Croque Monsieur – an easy and very popular hot sandwich

8 slices white bread – butter
4 slices Gruyère (or processed) cheese
4 slices ham
Mustard (Dijon if possible)

Butter the slices and make sandwiches by filling bread to the edges with a layer of ham and a layer of cheese to each sandwich. Heat some butter in a pan and fry the sandwiches until browned. Cover the pan with its lid during the final stages to melt the cheese. Spread mustard to taste on the outside of each sandwich. Serve the sandwiches piping hot, in paper towels. Accompany the snack with a Bull Shot – a can of Campbell's Beef consommé concentrate or mug of beef extract, heated and with a generous tot of brandy added to each shot.

This is a quick snack, full of warmth at the change of the night watch.

Section 5

PLANNING THE MENUS

Eating in an ever-changing environment

The debate as to the precedence of chicken or egg could be continued on the subject of planning for meals afloat. Should menus be considered first and stores adjusted accordingly, or should stores be purchased and the menus designed therefrom? Certain it is that what is not aboard cannot be cooked.

The prime consideration governing what is served for any meal afloat must be the weather. The dishes served to the crew after a rough passage in late autumn, after a spanking day's sailing in late spring or at the end of a lazy drift in high summer will be tuned to the needs of the hour. The curried beef which will provide central heating for a cold, wet and weary crew would not be appreciated in the indolence and somnolence which spreads over a cockpit in dead calm at the end of the afternoon's sun bathe, nor would a tuna salad with cream cheese refuel the crew at the end of the first shake-down trip of the season. To be successful the cook must ply his trade in the galley with one eye on the replenishment of the empty stomachs which sailing engenders and the other eye on the weather forecast and barometer. In preparation be prepared, ready for the sudden change from summer skies and a sailing breeze, to driving rain with too much foul wind and a cold wet crew. A bowl of soup with a dish of diced fried bread and a good mug of coffee laced with rum, can be the kiss of life to a cockpit under attack from wind and water. If hope can be revived, the faint hearted cheered, the strong restored in spirit by skill at the stove, the cook is worth his place in the boat.

As an omnivorous animal, man can eat at any time a great range of foodstuffs, but he rapidly declines on a limited diet. Restrictions of one kind or another can set in rapidly aboard a small cabin cruiser. Repetition induces monotony and, though the labels on the cans of prepared meals may portray a great variety of pictured delicacies (all in full colour), a reading of the small print below the picture will probably show a striking preponderance of potato flour, root vegetables and monosodium glutamate. These three plus colouring matter generally make up the greater part of the contents of most tinned meals. Even the 'lamb' of lamb casserole, the 'pork' of pork hash and the 'beef' of beef goulash may turn out to be textured vegetable protein from the soya bean. Mush is merely monotonous.

Food as fuel for the human machine

It is not without reason that many of those who have to cook afloat describe their crews as gannets or pelicans. This is not because of any resemblance to the birds' majestic sweep of wings on the wind, the controlled gliding search for prey, nor for the thrilling, death defying fish-hunting plunge into the sea. It is because of the great gape-distending swallow which follows the successful catch. The opening of an apparently bottomless pit vividly recalls the ever hungry crew whose ravenous open maws populate the nightmare of the ship's cook. This resemblance does not extend to the gannet's menu or the pelican's food which consists entirely of live fish, uncooked, untouched by human hand, unvaried and, for the bird, a balanced diet.

The human body requires food for four purposes, to provide the energy which powers movement, to supply the heat with which a normal physical temperature is maintained, to satisfy the needs for bodily growth and to replace cellular tissue destroyed by wear and tear, accident or illness. The food required for individual needs will depend upon three factors, age, activity and climate. The young consistently require more food than the aged for obvious reasons. Activity and climate are of particular importance in the cruising and sail-racing world. The sudden change from a possibly sedentary occupation within a heat controlled atmosphere to a vigorous participation in a physical activity exposed to wide fluctuations of weather, obviously demands a correspondingly dramatic change in food intake. Much of the enthusiasm which affects those who enjoy sailing probably stems from the unaccustomed pleasure of feeling hungry and eating with relish.

The balanced diet

The cult of slimming with its worship of the curve in the right place, its constant battle against the bulges in the wrong areas, and its catechism of the calorie count need not concern a sailing dietician, except to note that the calorie is the unit in which the nutritive value of food ingredients is measured as a heat energy source. Three sail changes in 45 minutes can make a heavy inroad into each crew member's calorie account. Of much greater importance is the consideration of the assortment of items, the make up of the menu as a fuel source for physical energy. The octane rating, so to speak, must be right for the efficient bodily combustion of food. The combined diet which provides a sufficiency for all requirements is called balanced and it will contain proteins, carbohydrates, vitamins, mineral salts and water.

The constituents of a balanced diet

The proteins, which are needed for cell replacement and growth are found in meat, fish, eggs, cheese, milk and soya beans. The carbohydrates are sugars and starches which, when broken down by digestion, provide heat and energy. Any excess carbohydrate not consumed by these two urgent processes is converted, to be stored as fat. Fats also provide heat and energy, and cold-weather diets should contain a high proportion of butter, margarine, meat, cream, nuts and oil. In addition to these three classes of ingredients, which form the largest part of a balanced diet, the maintenance of a healthy bodily condition requires minute quantities of two other food substances, the vitamins and mineral salts. The vitamins sustain the tone of the body functions, the mineral salts are essential to the cell structure of bones, teeth, blood and nerves. They are also involved in the acidity or alkalinity of the body fluids, the efficiency of the blood-stream transport system and the processes of digestion. The physical effects of deprivation of these trace elements are out of all proportion to their quantity in the total food intake. The records of the deficiency diseases, scurvy, rickets and beri-beri which decimated the ships' crews of the early circumnavigators are eloquent testimony, even today, to the importance of vitamins and mineral salts in our nutrition. Cooking processes have a direct effect upon them and much of the already minute quantity is broken down or dissolved in the preparation of the meal to be thrown away as waste.

The vitamins in fresh food

There are four main categories of vitamins, all of which are present in the raw material of foodstuff. Vitamin A, which increases resistance to infection and aids vision, is found in fish liver oil, in animal liver and in fresh dairy products. It is insoluble in water and is not affected by cooking processes. Carotine, found in yellow fruits and carrots is also converted to vitamin A by absorption in the body.

The vitamin B complex is a group of three vitamins which assist growth, help in the process of the conversion for energy and are particularly important to the nervous system. Found in whole meal, in yeast, milk, eggs, cheese and leafy vegetables, the vitamins B are soluble in water, are not destroyed by boiling unless the liquid is alkaline, but are broken down by frying, baking or canning processes. When boiling processes are employed in cooking green vegetables, bicarbonate of soda should not be used, and the cooking water should be kept to be incorporated in a sauce or gravy.

Vitamin C, possibly the most important, assists in the formation of red blood cells and aids the healing of wounds, broken bones and growth generally. It is soluble in water and is completely destroyed by alkalinity and boiling. Found in fresh fruit, salad vegetables and potatoes it is so easily lost that special care should be taken in their preparation. The ingredients should not be left to soak, should be prepared shortly before cooking, should be covered whilst cooking and boiled for the shortest possible period of time. Cooking under pressure preserves a greater proportion of vitamin C than does open saucepan boiling but, even so, much of the vitamin C will find its way into the cooking liquid. Some raw fruit every day is a certain method of obtaining the daily dosage of 'C'.

Vitamin D, found in fish liver oil and in dairy products, is also produced by the action of sunlight and a substance present in the skin. The most certain source of vitamin D is margarine, to which it is added at manufacture. Important as a factor in the growth and condition of teeth and bones it is not soluble in water and is unaffected by boiling temperatures.

The mineral salts in the balanced diet

The principal minerals needed for a healthy bodily function are calcium, iron, iodine, phosphorus, sodium and potassium. Eggs, milk, cheese, fish and green vegetables contain traces of all these. Though the quantities of the minerals absorbed are minute, the effect of their continued absence can be very serious. The condition of bones, of the blood stream, the glandular functions and the processes of digestion are all directly affected by these traces of minerals. All are soluble and though not changed by cooking processes, can be poured away with the waste cooking water. One of the commonest of minerals essential to our well-being is common salt. It is excreted with body perspiration and in prolonged periods of heat the salt loss may be considerable. In such climatic conditions salt tablets, obtainable at any druggist or chemist should be issued to the crew at regular intervals to make up the loss.

Fresh water

The essential and most vital element in a balanced diet is fresh water. It forms the major constituent of our cellular structure and upon its presence depends the whole of the digestive process and the transport, as solution, of the digested food material throughout the body. It is also the principal cleansing agent of our internal structure and waste is discharged, to be carried away in water, from our lungs at exhalation, from the skin by perspiration and via the kidneys at excretion. This constant water loss has to be replenished all the time while life continues. Deprived of this balanced intake of fresh water discomfort results. Continued deprivation produces physical collapse and, if the lack of fresh-water intake is prolonged, dehydration results in death. Any condition of thirst, no matter how desperate, is only made worse by drinking sea water. As a food material vital to life, fresh water has the highest priority in the diet.

A skeleton plan of a balanced diet

This then is the whole complex chemical equation which the cook must serve with material of the right quality and quantity, in the proper proportions at correct intervals, during the periods of exertion between waking and sleeping. The crew coming ashore at the end of a week-end's sailing or an offshore race or even a month's extended cruising holiday are unlikely to be toothless with scurvy, knock-kneed with rickets or blind with beri-beri. Even a bad cook could not achieve such devastation in so short a time. But they could certainly have suffered from indigestion, constipation, headaches, sickness and cramps, the causes for which could well be traced to their diet and the cook's activities. A daily balanced diet for an average adult should include:

Item	*Content*
1 pint fresh milk	first-class protein, fat, sugar, vitamins A, B, D, calcium, phosphorus.
3 oz. cooked meat or fish	first-class protein, fats, vitamin B, iron, calcium, iodine (in fish).
1 egg	protein, fat, vitamins B and D, iron.
2 oz. cheese	protein, fats, sugar, vitamin B.
½ lb bread (preferably wholemeal)	carbohydrate.
+ 1 helping cereal	vitamin B, calcium, iron.
1 serving potato + 1 serving green vegetables	carbohydrate, mineral salts, vitamins A, C.
+ 1 serving yellow vegetables	roughage.
+ 1 serving fruit	
2 oz. butter or margarine	fats, vitamins A, D, mineral salts.
2½ pints water (as tea, cocoa, coffee)	replacement of water loss.

Roughage

The contents of the vegetable items contain an ingredient of great importance to the well-being of those on board. Termed roughage, it consists of fibrous cellulose substances, totally indigestible and bulky, which stimulate intestinal excretion. The accumulation of waste in any process which uses energy will ultimately bring the production line to a halt. The physical condition of constipation is the body analogy to this situation. The presence of waste affects all the human reactions, physical and mental and speedily reduces efficiency in action. Important in any diet, roughage is needed in quantity and its absence will be quickly demonstrated by a change in the speed of response of physical alertness, as constipation develops. A serving of a heaped tablespoonful of bran, mixed with sliced banana, sugar and a cupful of milk at breakfast, every two or three days as a preventative, or the use of bran-containing breakfast cereals, is certainly preferable to the belated detonation in the gut produced by pharmaceutical dynamite.

The contribution to appetite of variety and appearance

To all the preceding components of the diet should be added one further item without which digestion is slow to begin, more particularly if the food fare consists largely of pre-constituted preserved material. An attractive appearance, a neat and colourful presentation and a pleasant aroma in a meal will encourage appetite and cause salivation, a very necessary precedent to the digestive process. The commonest and probably sincerest compliment paid to the cook and bestowed upon his handiwork is that it is mouth-watering. To achieve a standard deserving of such praise, the cook at the galley must include in his planned menus variety in colour and texture, some unusual local delicacies, the less common among ingredients, all of which will keep monotony at bay. This is the only sure way to avoid the daily appearance of the same old hash, that distasteful repetitive part of a sailing programme which converts what should be pleasurable eating into forced feeding. It should be the cook's prime concern to initiate the crew into the delights of the process of converting the ship's stores into cheerfully expended energy and effort.

Tapenade – an experiment in seasoning as a snack

8 hard boiled eggs
½ cup black olives
1 tin anchovy fillets
½ teaspoon mustard
1 tablespoon capers
1 tablespoon brandy
1 pinch pepper
Olive oil

Cut the hard boiled eggs in half and remove yolks. Soak anchovy in sufficient milk to cover, for 20 minutes (this will remove the salt). Mash yolks, fillets, mustard, olives, capers with brandy. Add olive oil in half teaspoonful at a time and continue to mash mixture to form a paste. Fill egg whites with the paste and serve with Cinzano Bianco, a slice of lemon and ice.

A cockpit snack while the crew are preparing ingredients for salad or a cabin snack while crew are preparing vegetables or a starter if visitors are dining aboard.

Section 6

FEEDING THE RACING CREW

Planning considerations

This section could well begin with the phrase 'So you want to try it the hard way,' because offshore racing is far removed from pleasure cruising. The predominant feature is no longer enjoyment, the accent is on achievement, because conditions which would keep the cruiser in port may well be just what the offshore racer prays for. Racing of this calibre has been likened by one addict of the game to standing naked to the winter wind under a cold shower whilst tearing up high denomination bank notes. This probably over-rates a little the hazards of offshore racing but it does point out two hardships common to those engaged in the sport: wetness and cold. The period of the race with a fast boat continuously driven hard by a fit crew, against all the uncertainties of weather and chances of misfortune represents an equation between the expenditure of human energy and the consumption of food by the body to replace that energy. Wet and cold in the equation weigh heavily on the debit side, warm and dry are profitable bonuses. The chances of success are improved by a favourable balance.

Offshore racing is not the only sphere of human activity in which men choose to fight a battle for survival, and the cook in a crew of an offshore racer cannot do better than study the manuals on survival produced by the medical branches of the armed services. Upon one salient feature all agree: planning, the most careful consideration, and preparation are essential in the face of hostile conditions. The cook then must plan the eating as carefully as the skipper schemes the sailing.

Consultation with the skipper

Three considerations will determine the ultimate stocking of food for the race.

1. The number in the crew
2. The duration of the race
3. The resulting weight of food and fresh water

The skipper will assess 1 accurately, and will give his opinion for 2 which will include an additional time factor in case of weather deterioration. It is the cook's responsibility now to work upon 1 and 2 and to come up with 3. Most of the constituents of the meal will be in dehydrated form, composite dishes, freeze-dried vegetables, dehydrated meat, milk, coffee, even instant puddings. The weight of water required to reconstitute such items must be set against that of cans as the alternative.

It is improbable that the skipper will ignore the effect of weight on his chances across the line, and lucky indeed is the crew who are permitted even a spare pair of socks. There will be fierce arguments about all those damned tins and an even more fearsome debate about the quantity of water needed to reconstitute dehydration. This latter always begins 'Can't you use sea water? You always put salt in the fresh water when cooking!' The problem is rarely resolved and compromise always triumphs. It is necessary to know the weight of stores and water so that the skipper may direct its stowage with hull trim in mind.

Fresh-water requirements

Fresh water ranks high in importance as a food item. Weighing some 10 pounds per gallon, it also poses a load problem. It is vital to life, a 10-stone man's body tissue and fluids contains 75 pints of water and, under energetic conditions, requires a daily intake of at least 2½ pints of water to replace normal losses due to exhalation, perspiration and excretion. More is required to keep the balance if the weather is hot and activity increases perspiration; even more is required if wind and salt spray whip the face and body for any length of time; much more is needed if sea sickness causes frequent vomiting. Economy may be exercised by using sea water for washing dishes and cooking vegetables or fish. It should be remembered that the boiling point of sea water is higher than fresh, 217° F (103° C), and that it contains some 6 ounces of salt per pint. If used for cooking vegetables, sea water needs to be diluted with three times its volume of fresh water. Despite all these savings, it will be found that when analysed, of the weight of food and water required for each man of the crew per day over half will be in water.

The advantages of dehydrated food material

Both in consideration of weight and in preparation of meals, dehydrated materials show a great advantage over their corresponding fresh constituents. The weight ratio is even further increased favourably if compared to canned items. Considerable progress has been made in the manufacture of freeze-dried materials. Complete composite dishes are available in packaged form and meals are available in great variety. The main meal of the day could range from chow mein or Indian curried chicken to Italian pizza or Mexican chilli con carne. The use of textured vegetable protein, a protein rich by-product of soya bean, is a ready substitute for meat, and solves both a weight and preservation problem. The range of meals which can be easily and quickly prepared is increased by the sauce and soup mixes, the milk powder, the dehydrated potatoes and onions and dried fruits all easily purchased. The weight and, sometimes more important, the volume of these foodstuffs can be further reduced if the contents of the packaging are removed and, together with the cut out directions, are sealed into labelled plastic bags.

The racing diet

The racing diet needs to be a high energy source so proteins, carbohydrates, sugars and fats will constitute a large proportion by weight of the food material. In planning the meals, the most nearly accurate method of calculating the quantity requirements is to work on a table of standard servings for an individual's daily food intake. The daily requirements per man of the more common food items are:

Milk	½ pint
Orange juice	⅓ pint
Eggs	1 (2 oz.)
Butter or margarine	2 oz.
Meat or fish	6 oz. fresh or 4 oz. preserved
Jam	1 oz.
Potatoes	3 oz.
Other vegetables: carrots, peas, beans, onions	4 oz. total
Dried fruit	3 oz.
Canned fruit	3 oz.
Bread	6 oz.
Breakfast cereal	2 oz.
Water	2½ pints

The sundry drink and cooking ingredients on the same basis (per man, per day) are:

Tea	¼ oz.
Cocoa	¼ oz.
Coffee	¼ oz.
Sugar	4 oz.
Instant milk (if used)	1½ oz.
Cooking oil or fat	½ oz.
Salt	¼ oz.

These ingredients would be spread over a programme of a substantial breakfast, a good lunch, in which the one hot item would be soup so as to limit the necessity for extensive cooking at midday and a hot substantial evening meal. Supper should be served at the changing of the night watch, the watch below eating before going on, the crew relieved eating as they come off for sleep. A hot soup in thermos flasks will revive cold, tired crew quickly during the night, especially if a glass of sherry per man is added to the ration. Snacks in the cockpit during the day are important to the intake of calories. Dried fruits, dates, apricots, prunes and sultanas, with slices of rich fruit cake will be enjoyed by the crew when the motion of the boat or the first race of the season may make other food distasteful.

The meals programme

Meal	*Item*	*Weight per man*
Breakfast	Fruit juice	
or	1 piece of fresh fruit	
	Bacon and egg	4 oz.
or	Sausage and tomato	4 oz.
or	Kippers	
	Bread, toast or crispbread	2 oz.
	Tea or coffee	10 oz. liquid
Forenoon snack	Savoury biscuits or cookies	1 oz.
	Fresh fruit juice	10 oz. liquid
Lunch	Soup	8 oz.
	Sandwiches	
	Bread	4 oz.
	filling meat or fish	3 oz.
	Tea or coffee or fruit juice	10 oz. liquid
Afternoon snack	Fruit cake	2 oz.
	Tea or coffee	10 oz. liquid
Dinner	Meat or fish	6 oz.
	Potatoes or rice	3 oz.
	Other vegetables	4 oz.
	Bread	4 oz.
	Cheese	3 oz.
	Tea or coffee	10 oz. liquid
Supper	Dried fruit	3 oz.
	Cake or chocolate	2 oz.
	Cocoa or coffee	10 oz. liquid

This programme provides a total weight of food and water per man per day of 7 lb. 1 oz. A crew of six racing for 3 days will consume 127 lb. 2 oz. of which total 67 lb. 8 oz. will be water. With some addition against extended passage time due to adverse weather conditions and the total weight of food and water to be carried, not counting the containers, will be some 175 lb., the equivalent of an additional crewman.

Realising the feeding scheme

Reduced to essentials the problem is one of energising sustained effort and mental alertness with stimulating warm food, prepared under difficult conditions by indifferently skilled individuals. It is unlikely that any one member of a racing team will be able to devote himself solely to the provision of meals. It is much more likely that everybody will take turns to cook, for cooking by watches enables the whole watch to be available at all times without calling those below. This distribution of the task of cooking calls for careful direction by the person responsible for the organisation of the provisions.

The first step towards success must be the minimising of the preparation of food items. The second step should be the reduction of the cooking processes involved to uncomplicated essentials. The third should be the simplification of service and consumption. The result must be a revitalised crew with a feeling of warmth at belt level, cheerfully prepared to continue to drive the boat to its utmost limits with efficiency and concentration.

Before the race, the canned, dehydrated and

packaged ingredients for each of the meals over the anticipated period are separated and set aside to be placed in plastic bags, gash-bin size. Clear directions for the preparations of the menu are enclosed and each bag is labelled with the meal and the day of use. At least one additional day is prepared. Each pack representing a meal can be drawn as a whole by the duty cook at the appropriate time. The cooking processes involved which should not be more than boiling, simmering or frying, are ascertained from the directions enclosed with the ingredients.

In addition to these prepared packs will be added at the last minute the fresh material, fruit, cake, bread, butter, milk and will be taken aboard for inclusion in the stores. The master cook should take aboard two cooked braises of meat, beef, lamb, chicken or rabbit in pressure cookers which will only need reheating. Two roast chickens well stuffed with sausage meat, some sliced ham, smoked sausage and smoked fish should be included to provide a variety of cold food for luncheon menus and snack sandwiches for the night watch. Two dozen hard boiled eggs wrapped in tissue can be stowed in the cook's deck boots against the skipper's weight-watching eye and the programme is off to a flying start. As near as prudent to the start, four wide-mouthed Thermos flasks should be filled with hot soup or stew.

These pre-race preparations will give the duty cooks little to do for the first two days but reheat and serve meals, which must be eaten in the cabin, never in the cockpit. The concentration of the crew and particularly of the helmsman must not be disturbed, and spillage of food and drink produces an obstructive mess. The duty cook will fill the hard-tack box in the cockpit with items from the meal pack in use so that each watch starts with its full quota of snacks to munch. The hot main meal of the first day will be served from the first pressure cooker. This will then become the main cooking pot since it has a locking lid, though there will be little need for pressurised processes in the reconstitution of dehydrated material. The second pressure cooker when emptied on the second day will be used to produce chicken soup from the carcases for the second night watch. From this point on, one pressure cooker should be kept going for hot soup alone, to maintain a constant supply for reheating.

When preparing and cooking meals, the duty cook should wear the cooking apron and oven gloves, for burned fingers and scalded hands reduce the crew by one immediately. The packaged meal ingredients should not present any difficulty. Directions for cooking times and quantities used should be followed closely and there is no need for the addition of a pinch of this or that to the prepared composite meal upon which the manufacturer has already spent much research and money. The aim of the exercise is to dish it up pleasantly as it is, with a prayer that it stays down. All cooking utensils must be locked to the fiddles when in use. Frying pans often present difficulties in this, but two wires stretched across the stove over the pan will usually hold it securely. It is the duty cook's responsibility to see that all used utensils and tableware are washed and stowed after the meal and that the gas is turned off at the cylinder.

Heavy weather feeding

From bitter experience sailing solo and from the accounts of those who have come through periods of full gale conditions in small boats, it is obvious that cooking in gale conditions, translated as the preparation of dishes to eat, is out of the question. Indeed, it is never in question, for the desire is not for food but for survival. Soup from a cooker, hot drinks from the kettle are the limit. Soup in half-filled bowls with bread or toast is the best answer to hot food and drink. Sandwiches of cheese with sweet pickle, cold meat and chutney may be prepared jammed in one's bunk. Drink is a necessity, hot and sweet if possible, especially for those who are seasick, to replace lost body fluid from vomiting. Brandy or rum in the drink is cheering, but if one is sick, it seems an awful waste. Inevitably battened down, it becomes a question of endurance and the resilience to ride it out.

For the real emergency, against the evil day of protracted gale conditions and its effect on the crew, a survival pack of self-heating cans, concentrated cereal and fruit blocks, glucose tablets and sealed water cans must be set aside. The contents of such emergency packs and their use is not the province of this book, which hopes to promote the joys of *living* afloat. The survival manuals of the armed services, the mountain rescue organisations and the institutes of medical research are the bibles for advice in this sphere. A good bookshelf with the writings of the great masochists who sailed alone across the oceans will encourage, during times of deadly despair in the face of the night of the sea, with the thought that it could probably be worse.

Bœuf à la bourguignonne – to take aboard.
(The finest beef stew in the world)

2 lb stewing beef (topside or shin)
½ bottle burgundy
1 glass brandy
1 large onion sliced
1 bouquet garni
12 small onions, whole
Beef extract cube
Butter and flour
½ lb mushrooms sliced
4 rashers streaky bacon
2 tablespoons oil

Marinade the meat, cut in large cubes, in the wine and the brandy, with the sliced onion and a bouquet garni. Leave for 3–4 hours. Take out the meat and brown on all sides in the frying pan with a little oil. Remove the meat to the pressure cooker. Put a little butter into the pan used for browning, heat and when the butter is melted stir in some flour to make a roux. Add sufficient beef stock made from the beef-extract cube to the roux and fry the small onions and mushrooms in the sauce for 15 minutes. Chop the rashers and add the bacon, sauce, onions and mushrooms to the pot. Strain the marinade and add to the contents of the cooker. Add salt to taste, bring cooker to pressure and cook for 35 minutes. Serve with assorted vegetables.

(For explanation of terms 'bouquet garni' and 'roux' see Herbs and Sauces sections.)

Section 7

THE DOMESTIC AMENITIES

The domestic comforts required for living afloat

The reality of the cruising, floating life is often a long way removed from the unimaginative world conjured up by the photographer for the yacht charter brochures. The semi-nude lovely stretched langorously on the sun-baked foredeck, the long legged beauty seductively spread over the cockpit, are artefacts produced under artificial sunlight on a mocked-up yacht in the pool of a film studio; even the sun tan is fake. If, however, the girl friend or the wife can be persuaded that she too can look like that on a boat, then life will take on a new dimension. But, and here lies the rub, actuality can obtrude very rapidly for it is upon the prosaic factor, the quality of the domestic arrangements that the success of family cruising depends. These personal comforts may be summed up as somewhere to sleep, somewhere to eat and sanitation somewhere. The standards required in the galley for good cooking are equally important in these three extensions of domestic life afloat, for happiness in life is not engendered by endurance and suffering.

Somewhere to sleep

The world-circling heroes of the sea, the lone sailors Robinson, Tabarly, Chichester, Alec Rose and Knox-Johnston possess a physical hardihood and resilience not usually present in the average family afloat. The capacity to relax amid a world in violent motion, to sleep in cold damp bedding, to wake undaunted by wet clothing are not the attributes of wives and children and are not always present in amateur sailing crews. Even over the comparatively short period of an offshore race the all male crew can find the lack of sleep more exhausting than sustained physical effort.

Much of the disturbance to sleep is due to the designed dimensions and situation of bunks.

Once flat on the back the individual becomes one with all the other objects aboard, the pots, charts, cushions and books, and can be as easily dislodged by the motion of the boat. Immobilisation of the body begins with the size of the bunk in width and length. Permanent single bunks, almost invariably installed in a fore and aft direction, need to be at least six feet in length, because some sailing men and women are that tall, and shorter crew members may fill the extra length with their kit bag. To be unable to relax by stretching limbs to their full extent is cramping purgatory not at all conducive to sleep. In width the single bunk should be no less than 2 ft. 6 in. and no more than 3 ft. Too narrow is just as uncomfortable as too short if one cannot choose to lie on one's back in indolent bliss. As thwart-ship motion predominates, too wide and one rolls uncontrollably from side to side. Permanent double bunks should not be installed in a fore-and-aft line for the same reason. The predominance of roll and the minimum width of 4 ft. make ample opportunity for the outside occupant to fall off. If installed thwart ship the rolling becomes head to toe rocking, which is cradle talk!

An alternative type of bunk is the pipe cot. A hybrid of the hammock, it consists of a length of stout canvas 6 ft. long and 3 ft. wide, one long-side of which is permanently fastened to the hull. The other side is attached lengthwise to a 3-in. diameter steel pipe. When this pipe is supported at its ends in notches on fore-and-aft bulkheads the stretched canvas provides a shelf upon which the would-be occupant makes a bed. Pipe cots have some advantages. First and foremost they can be stowed away, providing maximum sleeping accommodation only when needed. They can also be fitted one above the other in a 5 ft. headroom to sleep the crew in double tiers. The canvas of the cot is also easily dried if wet, much more so than a mattress.

Both bunks and pipe cots should be fitted with lee boards to secure the occupants in rough weather. In permanent bunks this could be a board 2 ft. wide and the length of the bunk, which can be fitted into bulkhead slots to form an outside retaining wall to the bunk. Another type of leeboard, which may be used with both permanent bunks or pipe cots is a strip of canvas 2 ft. wide and the length of the cot or bunk, fastened to the outside edge of the bunk base or pipe along its length. In use the strip is stretched upwards to the deck head by three spaced lines hooked to the cabin cross beams. When not in use canvas lee boards are easily stowed under the mattresses or rolled in the cot canvas.

Mattresses are usually of synthetic foam tailored to fit the bunks. The covers are generally of waterproof plastic fabric, durable and easily cleaned, but the cold surface of the plastic is apt to form a condensation plane to body warmth beneath the bedding. Such mattresses are improved if a loose canvas outer cover is fitted for sleeping, which increases warmth and minimises condensation. Pipe cots are rarely fitted with mattresses and woollen blankets are generally used as underlays. Warmth in bedding is engendered not so much by quantity of top cover as by resilient under thickness of insulation against heat loss between body and bunk. This insulation is provided by the air layer trapped within the bedding material. Thus the more fibrous the underlay and cover the warmer will be the occupant. Blankets for bedding should be chosen with this insulation in mind. Synthetic fibres are light and are easily aired but since water lies upon the surface of the fibre blankets and liners made of these materials they quickly feel damp. Woollen material is equally resilient and will absorb moisture in quantity before it feels damp.

Bedding popularly takes the form of sleeping bags in light-weight synthetic material. For that part of the sailing season when adverse weather conditions are the rule rather than the exception, choose warmer, though not necessarily heavier bags. The types used in mountaineering are excellent. Avoid bags with plastic waterproof covering. This traps the humid body-warmed air which cannot escape, and condensation and dampness invariably result. Sleeping bags should be aired on every possible occasion. One never knows when the next favourable chance will come.

Bag liners should always be used as they are easily washed or cleaned, much more so than the bag itself. If the weather is hot, cotton liners are advisable. The natural fibre absorbs perspiration and in high summer may be sufficient itself as bedding. So, too, pillow cases should be cotton for comfort.

Somewhere to eat

The cabin table which can at one and the same time accommodate a crew for meals, be transferred to the cockpit for an alfresco lunch, provide chart space for the navigator and, if required, fold up to increase sociability space in the cabin, has yet to be effectively designed. It appears, too, that where to put the table in the cabin space will never be resolved other than by compromise. The long tried traditional layout is to place the table in a fore-and-aft line in the middle of the cabin. This automatically demands that the table width must fold to at least a quarter of its extended size when not in use. The centre carcass upon which the flaps are hinged is hollow and provides drink storage. This layout requires settee seating in a fore-and-aft line on either side of the table. Seats of this design also provide sleeping space and, by rearrangement of the back-rest mattresses to the settee can convert seating for six into bunks for two on each side. Certainly the plan gives a spaciousness to the cabin and makes maximum use of the space for seating and sleeping. It does, however, invariably require the galley space to be moved either forward or aft of this area.

Many modern layouts embody a dinette arrangement with seating around three sides of a table set off to port or starboard of the saloon. This has one great disadvantage that when the crew is seated around the table, only the occupants of the two outside seats are free to move without disturbing the rest. If so required, the whole dinette complex may be converted, by a general upheaval of table, seats and mattresses into a double bunk. Considerable advance warning of this manoeuvre is necessary. The warmth of reciprocation to the suggestion 'and so to bed' may cool considerably before the somewhat complicated dormitory organisation is complete. In family circumstances the change from table to double bunk may be quite impossible without the total dislocation of the indoor sports, the large jig-saw puzzle, intricate collage or backgammon game in which the crew are engaged. In such cases it is usual for the owner to join the dog asleep in the cockpit. Hence the term 'dog house'?

There are some essential features which must be present in any table used afloat. First it must be firm and stable at all times. The rickety sway which affects so many folding models is an abomination. It must be large enough for the crew when sitting at table to have elbow room. Eating with the fresh air hungriness of life afloat demands a vigorous approach, free from neighbourly impediment and wave-engendered nudges. The table must be fitted with fiddles to prevent the motion of the table communicating itself to the tableware in unrestricted fashion. Fiddles, the raised surrounding rims to the table top must be at least 2 in. high, straight sided and hinged to the table edge. They can then be raised and fastened into position with bolts when circumstances demand. Heatproof laminates are the best material for cabin table tops, though there is much to be said for the contribution to décor made by polished or varnished mahogany table surface. The heatproof laminate then appears as table mats – which have to be stowed.

Sanitation somewhere

One can hear the old hands scornfully saying, 'What's wrong with a bucket?' Indeed there is little that can go wrong with a bucket, and no skin fittings, sea cocks, valves and pumps are required. In one respect it is superior to any water closet for it can be kept scrupulously clean and visibly so. Once, however, the family and mixed sexes comprise the crew, the females will not feel that their privacy is protected adequately by the command, 'All face aft!' as the bucket is prepared. So a marine water closet and, if possible, a separate loo compartment are commonplace today.

The designs are many and various. Those not pumping into retaining tanks use sea water for flushing, in most a double-action pump draws water and flushes on the same stroke; all need two skin fittings, one for entry and a larger for exit. Each must be fitted with a sea cock and it is advisable to turn these off if hard sailing, for sea water can pass the pump valves if sufficient force develops between wave and boat motion. The greatest drawback to what is in the family cruiser an absolute necessity, is the ease with which blockage of the pan can occur. The type using a large diameter diaphragm pump seems to suffer least. Any type with a multiplicity of valves gives hostages to fortune, for only the lightest toilet paper will flush with certainty. Crepe paper, paper towelling or newsprint is fatal to the operation and clearance of the blockage can be a very, very noisome task. If the stock of toilet paper is exhausted return to the bucket, for all else is fraught with the certainty of a bunged-up loo.

The separate loo compartment, a 'head de luxe' is a boon to life afloat in many ways. Always well ventilated, large enough for sitting, with a water supply and drainage to hand, it represents not only sanitation but privacy, a dressing room for feminity, and most usefully the coolest spot in the boat in hot weather. The loo pan's role as wine cooler, when frequently refilled with sea water, is well documented and as a cold store in which to hang cheese, smoked garlic sausage and salt fish, the heads has a range of uses other than its specific one. Since the sitting position demands a large space at low level, the unused area above and behind the w.c. pan is available for the fitment of a retractable washhand basin, which can be slid out of the way beneath the side deck when not in use. Filled from a kettle, the basin should be drained through the toilet to save skin fittings. If the basin outlet hose is passed through a hole in the w.c. pan lid, the waste water can be pumped away.

Little emphasis need be laid on the necessity for cleanliness, in this part of the ship especially. A regular scrub out to ensure that everything is clean round the bend is often one of the cook's perks, since he or she is well aware from their culinary activities of the need for scrupulous attention to a routine of cleanliness, both personal and in utensils, if contamination of a serious nature is to be avoided. Unfortunately the indiscriminate use of strong disinfectants can destroy pump washers and valves. A little goes a long way in the use of antiseptics and most makers issue instructions with their loo fitments which should be followed carefully. A reminder of the need for attention to cleanliness especially in energetic weather conditions can be exhibited in the loo. The recommendation reads 'gentlemen stand closer, it's further than you think'. 'ladies are requested to remain seated until the performance is completed'.

Sufferers from mal de mer should not take to the loo to be sick. Only a kneeling attitude before the pan can ensure that the target is hit. This position of obeisance before the might of wind and wave is best left to those with cast-iron stomachs. For the sea sick, plastic hand bowls should be provided. Light in weight, they are transportable, easier to use and much simpler to clean than the whole heads compartment.

Keeping warm

Personal warmth afloat starts with the right clothing, worn while sailing. While little or no problem in a summer season or in favoured latitudes, warmth can be a hard-won blessing in less kindly circumstances. Next to immersion, loss of body heat through exposure is one of the greatest hazards in sailing. The torso, however, is not the major area from which heat is lost. Medical research by the armed services has shown that 30 per cent of heat loss occurs from head and neck, 20 per cent from hands and wrists and 20 per cent from feet and ankles. The neck, wrists and ankles are areas where the blood stream runs nearest to the surface, the skin. These are the cooling areas of the human radiator. Cover these areas and a 70 per cent saving can result. The navy watch cap, a woollen scarf, two pairs of socks, the outer of wool, and woollen mitts with double cuffs will keep cold at bay.

Most synthetic fibres are lighter than natural material such as cotton or wool. As wind proofing and rain shedding, garments of man-made fibres, the anorak and windcheater, are superior. But as heat insulation particularly in wet conditions, wool is unbeatable. Natural wool garments will not wet through as quickly as will nylon or polyester (Terylene or Dacron), for wool will absorb 30 per cent of its own weight in moisture before it even feels wet. The rough fibrous surface of woollen material to a large extent prevents physical contact between garment interior and skin. The thick fibrous nature of the weave traps 80 per cent of its volume in air, a highly efficient thermal insulation layer. The rough hairy exterior surface of the natural wool jersey or jacket facilitates the formation of droplets of water and absorbs the energy of impact of rain or spray so that water does not penetrate quickly into the weave. Wool has a high absorption capacity for water and with it the physical phenomenon of heat of absorption which actually dries out the fibres. If woollen underclothes have got wet in sailing, the quickest method of drying them is to roll into two woollen blankets in the wet garments, all standing, get into the sleeping bag and all will dry out rapidly. Sweaters and blankets of natural wool should not be washed or dry cleaned until they make their presence known to the nose. The natural oil, so important to the physical properties of the fibre is removed in washing and cleaning. The addition of three tablespoons of olive oil to a gallon of rinsing water will replace some of the lost natural oil. All these warming facts have been known to the long haired, woollen coated, mountain sheep for centuries. From the old tup, cud chewing in a wild mountain gale, take a tip. Sew a double layer of thick woollen cloth into the seat of your favourite pair of sailing trousers. It will keep this performance-sensitive area alert in the worst conditions of cold.

Warmth for the boat interior can be achieved by using a cabin heater system. There are types using pressurised gas fuel, paraffin, diesel oil and solid fuels. Each and every one has its own specialty, all have one factor in common, they need ventilation to the open air. The drowsy fug of an overheated underventilated cabin is a certain source of headaches and general malaise, and emergence from such a debilitating atmosphere to the freshness of cold air is more shocking than bracing. Heat then by all means, but don't hermetically seal the cabin. All space heaters should be secured to the cabin structure, even those portable types with fail-safe extinction on upset, for though the fuel is cut off the heater itsef is still hot and can cause burns or start a fire.

Keeping dry

This naturally follows keeping warm, for the chill of sailing is usually accompanied by wet conditions. The greatest drying agent available afloat or ashore is the movement of air, a breeze, a wind, a gale. Unfortunately these atmospheric movements are almost universally associated with rain or spray at sea. The interior of the cabin should be kept dry for as long as possible and in spite of adverse conditions. This implies that water and wet gear must be kept out. The rain- and spray-soaked heavy sailing gear should not be allowed into the cabin. A wet locker should be accessible from the dog house or cockpit so that rain- or spray-soaked gear can be hung in the locker before entering the cabin. This locker which should be lined, drained and waterproof, will, if well ventilated, dry modern sailing clothes, most of which come as drip dry material. Such clothes should not go into the cabin wet.

Underclothes which have been soaked by weather need to be hung to dry. A net stretched over the galley at ceiling level is better than clothes lines. It enables wet articles to be spread out to dry and so avoids the inconvenience of hanging obstructions. The galley stove with its associated ventilation system will soon dry out the gear. The presence in the cabin of wet clothes hung to dry will increase the general dampness and condensation. Even in heavy weather the ventilation of the interior of the boat should be kept going unless water threatens to enter where the damp atmosphere from inside is making an exit. The cooker will combine its function of providing hot soup with drying out wet garments. But soaked clothes, too wet to hang in the cabin, should be put into plastic waterproof bags. At the next opportunity they can be hung in the air to dry. If there is an accumulation of wet clothing it is better to keep it apart in waterproof bags rather than create a dripping mess and wet atmosphere in what should be the dry spot on the ship.

Savoury scramble

2 tablespoons milk
1 oz. butter
1 tablespoon chopped parsley
3 rounds buttered toast
2 Gruyère cheese portions, chopped finely
3 eggs, beaten
Salt and pepper to taste

Heat together milk and butter. Add beaten eggs until beginning to set, fold in the cheese and parsley and season with salt and pepper. Scramble the mixture while cooking, and pile on hot buttered toast. Serve immediately.

Section 8
ENTERTAINMENT

The social side of cruising

Traditionally the sailor, a long voyage over, was ready at the slightest provocation for fun and games ashore, with a heavy accent on wine, women and song. This happy syndrome was a reaction born of the harshness of the 18th-century naval discipline and the lack of shore leave. It is kept alive by the 20th-century yachtsman, who can conjure up a burning desire for conviviality, not on years or even months of salt beef and weeviled ship's biscuit, but on 6 hours of salt water and a smart sailing breeze. As sailors we are a happy breed, and it only requires an anchorage or a port with two or more similarly biased individualists gathered together and entertainment looms large on the horizon. The skipper on the prowl around the quays and pontoons is liable from an overwhelming feeling of bonhomie to invite the company of all the crews assembled to a party aboard his boat that very evening. Undeterred by any preoccupation with the amount of alcohol or even the number of glasses aboard, he will undoubtedly expect the programme at 18.30 hours to be all that his flag and his burgee desires. The problems of extending $\frac{1}{2}$ bottle of gin, 1 bottle of white wine (vin de very small table), 2 lemons and 6 tonics to several rounds of drink, eight to the round, he confidently leaves to the cook, so help him or her.

Vinegar, poured into an empty wine bottle with the addition of a teaspoonful of paint thinners was one cook's answer to just such a problem. The concoction, served first as a sip 'from the retsina we bought back from the Ionian last year', sent the company ashore where supplies were inexhaustible. Such ploys can, however, impair the owner's reputation.

Entertainment demands versatility. The resourceful cook will not need subterfuge and will soon have the emergency, the party, well in hand. Drawing upon those supplies carefully stowed and labelled 'in spite of the skipper', the cognac (medicinal reviver), the rum (heavy weather warmth), the whisky (external and internal antiseptic), from the medicine chest, the orange juice (anti scorbutic), the lemons (vitamin C), from the first aid box, the cherries, the cloves, nutmeg and mace and the miniature liqueurs from the flavouring locker, the expected excellencies to confound the sceptics will be produced. For entertainment, like bad weather, is not a case of 'if' but of 'when', and the necessities required in the face of such certain hazards should be to hand. Just as good seamanship and expertise under sail are indicative of a well-found vessel and a well-schooled crew, so the originality and character of a vessel's entertainment are a measure of the ability of the cook and a gauge to the style of the ship's company. An over-large gathering in an undersized cockpit, with a rapid hand out of warm beer and a mug of peanuts does not constitute entertainment worthy of the name. The number of floating cans which precedes dispersal is also an indication of slack gash discipline on the part of those involved.

A suggested formula for a successful party

Entertainment on board should have a character born of a common interest in the sea and derived from a love of sailing. Its individuality will stem from the skipper, the crew and their experience of the floating world. Entertainment on boats bears no resemblance to land-based picnics or house-based jollifications in competition with the Jones, Browns and Robinsons on a social roundabout. It can be successfully achieved by two on a four-tonner and yet a total failure for a dozen or more on a TSD floating gin palace with a paid crew of three. The successful party afloat, particularly in summer, can be organised to a simple formula upon which the cook devises the programme. It is:

(1) a warm welcome
(2) cold drinks
(3) 'up spirits'
(4) aperitifs, cups and punches
(5) attractive, tasty snacks
(6) a local specialty
(7) disposable tableware and cutlery
(8) heavy based glasses
(9) the guests do the talking
(10) speeding the parting guests

Since eating at such a gathering is a hand to mouth affair, numbers 6, 7 and 8 are most important.

A warm welcome

The warmth of the welcome is really measured in the number of guests. Do not oversell the accommodation, for the overcrowded gaggle on a small boat is not amusing. To find oneself, on the only seat available, consuming warm red vino in the loo may be funny 'peculiar' but it is not funny 'Ha! Ha!'. Real social pleasure is found in space for enjoyment, space to chat, to drink, to eat delicately, and space is most important. So gauge the boat in social tonnage/cubic measure as well as in registered tons. A favourite solution to party accommodation, particularly when anchored or on trots is to raft up, with three or four boats moored abreast of each other and the party spread over the assembled cockpits. All the preparations must be complete before the first of the guests arrive. A warm welcome cannot be extended if the hard boiled eggs are half stuffed.

Cold drinks

First considerations are the possibilities for refrigeration and alternative cooling methods. Cold drinks are no problem to the boat with a refrigerator or ice-box. As a solution to the problem of chilling and ice for drinks, the refrigerator is not as simple as all that. The craft with a waterline of 25 to 30 ft. will be able to accommodate a small refrigerator with a storage capacity of 1½ cubic ft. The external dimensions of such a container are within the 16 in. deep, 24 in. high and 18 in. wide range. If electricity powered a compressor some 6 in. × 15 in. × 9 in. will be additional. An electric 'fridge of such a size will draw some 4·5 amps and battery capacity and charging facilities will be needed to provide this power of some 50 watts. If installed, the refrigerator makes a useful extension of galley top space and should be placed between stove and sink. Other 'fridges, powered by pressurised gas fuel or kerosene need ventilation to the open air and have to be installed with this in mind. Both types work on adiabatic expansion cooling, are temperature controlled by operation of fuel valve with a pilot burner and fail-safe mechanism. The gas operated variety is suspect by some, since the pilot light is a source of danger to gas leaking from equipment other than the 'fridge. A popular installation site for gas refrigerators in motor craft is under the helmsman's seat, in the cockpit or dog house. No design for an attached parachute has yet been fitted to this potential ejection mechanism. Most small craft must rely on other methods for cooling drinks.

The ice-box is one such alternative, space for space is more economical than a powered 'fridge, and has the advantage that most models are transportable. All, however, require ice as the cooling agent. Most fishing ports have factories from which ice may be bought, a bucket full at the time, for use with the ice-box. Do not, repeat not, never, never buy ice from the fish market. It always smells, not of fish since fresh fish has no smell, but of the market. It will produce in the cabin or cockpit the atmosphere of the market from whence it came, which is no place for a party. Ice in moulded pieces may also be bought from the marina or the café ashore. It may be necessary to buy a bottle of vermouth for the bar tender as well, but as ice for drinks it is easier to serve than the broken ice achieved by battering the canvas-wrapped block with a starting handle. Broken or moulded ice pieces will remain separate if a squirt of soda water is played over them in the ice bucket.

Chilling is not impossible without ice. Bottles wrapped in soaked towelling and hung in the shrouds exposed to the wind will cool by the process of evaporation. The towelling must be kept damp with sea water. Drinking water may be chilled by the same process if hung in a canvas flagon or bucket in the breeze. Directions for making such a cooling canvas container will be found in any of many books on seaman's crafts and rope work. Wine and vermouth may be cooled if the bottles, in nylon mesh bags, are lowered to three or so fathoms in the sea, except in the Gulf Stream or off an atomic power station outfall. In all the following descriptions of mixtures and cocktails it should be assumed that ice will be included in the concoction. If ice is not necessary, the recipe will say so.

'Up Spirits'

Ogden Nash summed up the need for spirits, both high and alcoholic, at a party in the epigram 'Candy is dandy but liquor is quicker'. The production of alcohol, innocently discovered in man's infancy, has alternately fermented joy and trouble ever since. One of the earliest names given to the distilled liquid result of a micro organism yeast, was aqua vitae – the water of life. This well-deserved title has been much modified by linguistics through the centuries, from aqua vit to eau de vie or uisge beatha, but its enlivening effect continues unchanged. The familiar result of the call 'Up Spirits' is a merry crew, and the taking of these lively waters will be the initial theme of shipboard entertainment. A varied selection should be available to give predilection time to enjoy addiction. The spirits for the guests aboard will be chosen from brandy, whisky, rum, gin, vodka and, if the boat is so based, could well include localised varieties such as tequila, oozu or arak. The last has been used in emergency as cooking fuel.

Brandy

The name is derived from the 17th-century 'brandwein' of Europe, so called because the wine was burned or distilled to produce the spirit. Production requires two stages, the fermentation of grape juice and a double distillation of the ferment. It is well documented that good wine makes poor brandy, whereas poor wine can make excellent brandy. It is made in most of the wine producing countries of the world. Europe, Australia, the Americas and South Africa all produce brandy. California makes more than France.

However, most often when one speaks of brandy, the reference is to a French brandy and to Cognac at that. Cognac is a blended spirit produced from the local wine of the area around the town of Cognac in the Charente district north of Bordeaux. Another distinctive brandy is Armagnac, named after the district west of Toulouse whence it derives. It is always aged in the wood for long periods, twenty years or more, and superb examples are prized above Cognac. Calvados, a brandy from Normandy is distilled from the cider for which this part of France is famous. It closely resembles the Southern Comfort of St Louis, Missouri, or the old fashioned applejack of New England, a glass of which was aptly described as 'a slug of blue fish hooks'. Such has been the influence of France upon the brandy world that in Spain the word for the spirit is Conac. This has a distinctive flavour, a national taste and a more powerful aroma, and is extensively used in the production of sherry. Brandy once bottled ceases to improve and can only deteriorate by evaporation of the alcohol. The many designations of supposed quality proclaimed by the labels on bottles are to be regarded with suspicion. Beware stars, XO (extra old), cordon bleu, medaillon Napoléon (III not Bonaparte), and even dates of years, which may only refer to the age of the cask.

Good brandy is expensive, fine quality brandy should be treated with the respect it deserves. There is no need to warm (with hot water) the glass in which it is served. Presented in a snifter of moderate size, the warmth of the cupped hands will release the bouquet which will reach the nose, sharpening the palate before the liquid is tasted. Such excellencies should not be debased by additives. As Charles Lamb said 'To add water to brandy is to spoil both,' and this applies to all fine spirits with a characteristic flavour. Ordinary commercial brands are a suitable base for mixed drinks.

The most widely known of the mixtures based upon brandy is from the great cocktail era of the early 1920s.

The Sidecar
In proportion $\frac{1}{2}$ brandy, $\frac{1}{4}$ lemon juice, $\frac{1}{4}$ Cointreau. Mix, shake well, strain and serve.

A mix using Calvados is aptly named:
Apple Jackrabbit
$\frac{1}{2}$ oz. Calvados, $\frac{1}{2}$ oz. lemon juice, $\frac{1}{2}$ oz. orange juice, 1 teaspoon grenadine syrup. Mix, shake well, strain and serve.

The **'B and B'** is a mix of equal parts of Cognac and Benedictine liqueur.

A mixture nautically known as:
Between the Sheets or **Out of Stays**
is a mixture of $\frac{1}{3}$ cognac, $\frac{1}{3}$ white rum and $\frac{1}{3}$

Cointreau. Progress is liable to be limited by too many of these.

A mixture of fruit brandies with champagne has been called, in honour of its happy timely invention,

Royal Wedding
In these proportions ¼ kirsch, ¼ orange juice, ½ peach brandy. Mix, shake well, strain and top up with champagne.

Whisky

First made by the Irish eight hundred years ago (when it is spelled whiskey), adopted by the Scots and christened in the Gaelic translation of 'the water of life', uisge beatha, it is from the mispronunciation of this last that the name whisky derives. Popularised in the 19th century by the Balmoral set led by Queen Victoria, dear Albert, and her whisky addicted loyal servant John Brown, Scotch as it is now universally known has colonised the world. Its distinctive flavour is variously attributed to the water source from burns (the streams not the poet), to the peat fuel used in the warming of the malt, to the oak sherry casks used in the maturing process and to so many other trace elements that some may well have come from the heavy breathing of excise men.

Whisky is the result of a triple stage process, first the production of malt, then the fermentation of this and finally the distillation of the spirit from the ferment. Single malt whisky is the sole product of an individual distillery and is made by a single distillation from a pot still. Grain whisky is produced by the continuous distillation in a coffey still, fractions being withdrawn at stages to be returned for further distillation. Blended whisky is a mixture of both types. Irish whiskey, which has a quite distinctive flavour is produced in a manner akin to Scotch. The individuality of the flavour derives from the early addition of oats to the malt. Discussion as to the differences in quality between Irish whiskey and Scotch are best left to the Irish and Scots. Not for nothing did the Japanese rechristen the village which attempts to make whisky, 'Aberdeen'.

Whiskey, with an 'e', is also distilled in two types in the United States and in Canada, both as straight and as blended products. Its arrival in both countries had to await the Irish/Scottish immigrant tide. As Rye, which should contain 51 per cent rye, or Bourbon which should contain 51 per cent corn, it is manufactured in vast quantities not all of which are legally recognised. Bourbon is so named after a county in which it was first made, when a Baptist minister, God bless him, set up a still in Georgetown, Kentucky. After distillation of the mash the addition of a neutral spirit produces a lighter bodied liquor which is then matured in charred white oak casks.

Additives to Scotch are regarded by many as sacrilege and in the case of a single malt, rightly so. A popular treatment enjoyed by some Scotch drinkers is to serve whisky on the rocks. The liquor is poured into a glass containing broken ice. Dilution then depends upon speed of consumption, the warmth of the hand on the glass or the climate. Some less orthodox mixtures with whisky as a base are:

Blood and Sand
Mix ½ oz. each Scotch whisky, cherry brandy, orange juice, sweet vermouth. Shake well, strain and serve.

With other whiskeys make:

Manhattan
Mix 1 oz. Bourbon, ½ oz. dry vermouth and a dash of angosturas. Shake well and serve with a cocktail cherry.

Fancy free
Mix 1 oz. rye whiskey, a dash of orange

bitters, a dash of angostura bitters and 2 dashes of maraschino. Shake well and serve.

There are no snakes in Ireland, but St Patrick would have considered the following a substitute poison no doubt.

Serpent's tooth
Mix 1 oz. Irish whiskey, 2 oz. sweet vermouth, 1 oz. lemon juice, ½ oz. kummel and a dash of angostura bitters. Shake well and serve.

Three old favourites made with blended Scotch are:

Whisky mac
Half and half by proportion blended Scotch and ginger ale. Do not add ice.

Whisky sour
Mix 1 oz. blended Scotch, juice ½ lemon, 1 teaspoon sugar. Shake well, strain and serve.

Finally in the name of the ancient Anglo-Scottish-French alliances:

The Bunny hug
Mix equal parts of Scotch, London dry gin and Pernod, quarante cinq. Shake well, serve very cold. Such a hug could only come from a bare bunny, at the Moulin Rouge.

Rum

Rum has the distinction among spirits that its varieties differ in flavour according to their place of origin and not to their ingredients, for all rum is made from cane sugar, even its name is derived from the Latin for sugar, saccharum. The spirit originated in the West Indies and still retains its local tastes. That from Jamaica is usually dark, pungent and strong, the rum from Barbados and Trinidad is lighter and drier. Demerara in Guyana produces an ultra light spirit. The white rums come from Cuba and Puerto Rico, Daiquire and Baccardi respectively, while the Lesser Antilles, Martinique and Guadeloupe produce the softer 'grand arome' St James rum, as one would expect from a French district. The greater part of the world's rum comes from Puerto Rico and the United States of America.

Rum was a New England industry in the early 18th century. The raw material, molasses, was a cargo carried from the West Indies in fast Boston sailing traders. Their triangular round trip consisted of a leg from Boston to Europe and Africa with rum, from Africa to the West Indies with slaves and a final leg from the islands to Boston with molasses. The imposition of taxes on the imported molasses infuriated the colonists of New England and probably contributed as much to secession as did the Boston teetotal party. Certainly rum played a significant part in two American historic episodes. It is said that Paul Revere rode morosely and withdrawn on his famous ride at first, but after stopping at a rum distillery run by one Isaac Hall he galloped off furiously shouting 'The English are coming.' George Washington's election as President too is rumoured not to be due so much to inspired electorial campaigning but to seventy-five gallons of rum distributed gratis among the electorate. Even today the rums carry labels alluding to the past history of the trade, though the quality of liquor which preserved Nelson's remains is no longer with us.

Of rum mixes the names of the following perpetuate some of the former greatness of the spirit.

Captain's Blood
Mix 1 oz. Jamaican rum, 2 teaspoons unsweetened lime juice and a dash of angostura. Shake well, strain and serve.

Planter's Punch
For a cane baron's drink mix 2 oz.

Jamaican rum, 1 oz. lemon juice, 1 teaspoon grenadine syrup and a dash of angostura. Stir into crushed ice, top with soda water, decorate with rounds of lemon, serve with a straw.

The 18th-century New England fishermen used this cold punch as insulation against wind and weather:

Fishhouse Punch
1 bottle Jamaican rum, ½ bottle brandy, ¼ lb brown sugar (Demerara), 2 teaspoons peach bitters, 1½ pints soda water. Pour the mixture over ice in a bowl and serve.

From Martinique comes this truly French rum mix:

St James elixir
In proportion mix ½ St James rum, ¼ Cointreau, ¼ framboise (raspberry liqueur) top up with bitter lemon. Decorate with lemon rind, twist and serve with a straw as a long drink.

Vodka

Vodka, spelled in a large number of ways for so few letters, has a legendary origin in Russia. It is more probably a Polish invention and, botanically flavoured, was served as a medicine, Zubrowka. Vodka is one such available today, coloured pale green by the infusion of aromatic Zubrowka grass. Some say it smells of fragrant hay fields in May, others remark upon its stable origin, but such rarer imported vodkas are not intended as ingredients for mixtures. Distilled from grain spirit, they deserve to be flattered, served unadulterated, swallowed at one gulp, but not necessarily accompanied by the tinkle of broken glass.

Modern vodka is Russian only by inference of name. Smirnoff Vodka is American through and through. The spirit is distilled in vast quantities in the United States of America and England, contains no medicinal ingredients or additives and is tasteless and scentless. Straightforward domestic brands are suitable for mixtures such as:

Bloody Mary
Mix 1 oz. Vodka, 1 small can of chilled tomato juice, a dash of celery salt, a dash of red pepper and a teaspoon of Worcester sauce. Serve, it need not be iced.

Tasting only of tomato and spices, its punch is not observed until too late. The same mixture with Tequila substituted for vodka is known as **Sangre Maria**. Both mixes speak an international language.

If your companion for breakfast is a man-sized hangover, the **Russian Bull Shot** may help. Mix a can of Campbell's condensed beef consommé, 2 oz. vodka, juice of half a lemon, a dash of red pepper and a teaspoonful of Worcester sauce. Serve, to be swallowed rapidly, as a medicinal draught.

Two vodka varieties of well-known whisky mixes are less Russian than their titles.

Balalaika
Mix in proportion 1 oz. vodka, ¼ lemon juice, ¼ Cointreau and a twist of orange peel. Serve chilled.

Moscow Mule
1 oz. vodka. 2 oz. green ginger wine. 1 oz. campari. Shake and serve chilled.

Gin

Gin, distilled from rye and flavoured with juniper berries was first produced by the medical school of Leyden, Holland, in the 15th century, its name being derived from the Latin for juniper, ginevra. The first recorded distillery for gin was set up in 1575 at Amsterdam by Lucas Bols, still a famous name in gin. By the 18th century the underpaid, half starved labouring population of England, in a state of gin-sodden intoxication, slaved their lives away under their ruling lords and masters, themselves in a costlier condition of inebriation from brandy, to build the greatest empire the world has ever known. 'Drunk for 1 penny, dead drunk for tuppence, straw for nothing' advertised the gin palaces, immortalised by Hogarth in 1751. Not for nothing was gin labelled 'Mother's Ruin' or 'Cuckold's Comfort'.

Its anti-social image and its purity both now refined, modern gin has two forms, the London Dry type and the more aromatic Plymouth or Hollands. Vast quantities are distilled in England, Holland and the United States of America, the greatest quantity of London Dry being made in Peoria, Illinois. To the neutral grain spirit is added juniper, coriander and an accompanying tribe of berries and barks. The nature of these additives may be ascertained by placing a few drops of the gin on the back of the hand. Rub gently to evaporate the alcohol and the scent of the heavier flavouring oils will remain. Though not an after-shave lotion, gin is a very good external antiseptic.

Two famous gin-based drinks have survived from its murky past, the John Collins and the Pink gin. The first was recommended by the military in the days of the British Raj and the second was dispensed by the seafaring quacks in sail. Their 19th century popularity as drinks has not waned in either camp.

John Collins
Mix 1 oz. dry gin, ½ tablespoon white sugar, juice of half a lemon. Shake, strain, pour over cracked ice and top with soda or tonic water.

Pink gin
Shake a few drops of angostura bitters into a wine glass and roll around the glass. Throw out the excess. Over cracked ice add 1½ oz. Plymouth gin to the glass and top with soda water.

Gin is the most popular spirit base upon which to produce mixed drinks for a party. An early reference to a mix composed of gin, sugar, bitters and water as a cocktail occurs in *The American Journal* of 1806, and the now famous *Bartenders' Journal* of 1882 compiled by Harry Johnson refers to many cocktails as mixes in a modern style. Certainly Harry's New York Bar at 'Sank roo doe noo' in the Paris of the 1920s originated many of the cocktails still popular today.

A small selection, all of which need ice is:

Bronx
Mix in proportion ½ dry gin, ¼ sweet vermouth, ¼ dry vermouth, juice of a quarter of an orange. Shake, drain and serve.

Gimlet
Mix in proportion ½ dry gin, ½ lime juice cordial. Shake, strain and serve.

Negroni
Mix 2 oz. dry gin, 1 oz. sweet vermouth and 1 oz. campari. Pour over ice and add soda water to taste. Decorate with a slice of orange.

Silver streak
Mix in proportion ½ dry gin, ¼ lemon juice, ¼ kummel. Shake, strain and serve.

White Lady
Mix in proportion ½ dry gin, ¼ lemon juice, ¼ Cointreau, 1 teaspoon egg white. Shake, strain and serve.

The cocktail which has attained a mystique all of its own is the Dry Martini. Its addicts argue endlessly over the proportions of its ingredients, the type of ice to be used, whether to shake or to stir and even in which direction to stir. Volumes have been written about the subtleties of putting together a portion of gin with a portion of dry vermouth. Famous makers of dry vermouth quote the proportions as 3 of gin to 1 of vermouth. 'Not a dry martini,' reply the aficionado. Friendships have been broken and divorces obtained over the ratios of gin to vermouth. These range from 12 of gin to 1 of dry vermouth to 7 of gin to 1 of dry vermouth. Some fill the glass with crushed ice, pour in a measure of vermouth, allow to stand for 30 seconds before draining off, then top up with gin; there are even those who pour the gin, bow towards Paris and drink the result as a dry martini. The common ground for all this argument is that dry martinis should never be consumed in the singular.

The aperitifs and vermouths

A shipboard party on spirits alone closely resembles the puissance event in show jumping competitions. As round follows round the fences become more and more formidable and the participants less and less. So if the entertainment is not to conclude amid the bodies of the fallen, some drinks of a less formidable character must be provided. Sherry and the various vermouths, popular constituents of cocktails, may be served alone as aperitifs much appreciated by those who prefer milder party drinks.

Vermouth as a medicinal draught of aromatic wine, brewed with herbs and spices was known to the Greeks of 5 BC. Reincarnated by an Italian in Germany, renamed for the wormwood which was its principal herbal additive, it has been adopted by the Italians and French to be rechristened with a number of brand names. The sweet and dry Martinis of Italy and France, the dry Noilly Prat, the very dry French Chambery and the bitter Campari are a few of these. As aperitifs, the preludes to gracious eating, the recipes for which are jealously guarded secrets, Byrrh, Dubonnet and St Raphael are known the world over. Each and every one makes a pleasant drink, served as a measure with a slice of lemon or orange and a generous portion of ice. A popular mixture of the vermouths is known as:

Americano
Mix in proportion $\frac{1}{3}$ campari and $\frac{2}{3}$ sweet vermouth. Pour over ice. Serve with a twist of lemon peel.

There are aperitifs of a different origin, the successors to the deadly absinthe, which are most popular for lunch-time socials, the Pastis and Pernods. Distilled from the staranis pod Pastis is the name of the famous aperitif closely associated with the great port of Marseilles. It has a characteristic reaction with water and, as Pernod quarante cinq, colours milky pale green with water. The other equally well-known varieties are Ricard or Berger, distilled with spirit from the liquorice, which with water become milky white. Both are poured over ice before dilution with water.

Liqueurs

Since liqueurs are much in evidence in mixed drinks and are also very useful as flavouring additives to desserts and fruit salad, the following examples as miniatures could be included in the cook's stores.

Benedictine D.O.M. Deo optimo maximo
The Benedictine monks' tonic, with every sip a thanksgiving, brandy based, its composition is still secret.

Chartreuse
The Carthusians' answer to their clerical Benedictine brethren. Yellow or green in colour, the green is the stronger, now produced in Spain on a brandy base.

Cointreau and Curaçao
An orange-flavoured liqueur from the island of Curaçao based on rum and distilled with the local island oranges. Both are sometimes known as Triple Sec.

Crème de Menthe and Cuisenier
The green peppermint liqueur with a strong female following.

Crème de Framboise
The raspberry-flavoured liqueur from France much used in dessert ice cream.

Grand Marnier
This is the great orange brandy of distinctive flavour.

Kummel
A distillation of spirit with caraway seeds, originating in Germany and the Baltic States.

Strega
The Italian liqueur distilled with citrus fruit and herbs.

Tia Maria
Rum based, this is the coffee liqueur of the West Indies. A mixture in which the liqueur predominates is made from equal portions of Kummel and dry gin – supposedly called a 'gummel'.

Cups and punches

If the weather is very hot, ice-cold long drinks suitable for thirst-quenching consumption and scaled to a more moderate alcoholic standard are advisable.

A typical cup is made from:

> 1 bottle of champagne, 1 bottle soda water, 1 liqueur glass Curaçao, 2 tablespoons white sugar, 1 orange sliced thinly. Ice in quantity is added to the required amount made in the proportions above.

A cup with more body alcoholically is made from:

> 1 bottle dry sherry, 1 bottle champagne, 1 bottle soda water, 1 liqueur glass Strega, 2 tablespoons white sugar, the thin rind of a lemon. Mix and add ice in quantity.

Two punches made from wine mixtures and fruit to be served cold are:

> **Sangria**
> 1 large bottle red wine ($1\frac{1}{2}$/2 litres), 2 lemons in thin slices, 6 peaches in thin slices, rind of 1 large cucumber, 2 bottles of tonic water. Ice in quantity added when serving.
>
> **Limonyada**
> 1 bottle white wine, 1 bottle red wine, $\frac{1}{2}$ lb white sugar, 1 bottle soda water, the thin peel of six lemons, 1 liqueur glass Strega. Ice in quantity added when serving.

Both Sangria and Limonyada need to stand after preparation for some hours for the flavour to develop. Skippers please note and order in advance.

Attractive tasty snacks

The essential characteristic of snacks for guests on board must be the simplicity of their preparation. The elaborate party confections, the delicacies in aspic and the jellied delights of a land-based cocktail rout are not for the cockpit. The golden rule must be to keep it simple at all costs; even if it is smoked swordfish, roll it up and impale it on a cocktail stick. Eating at a party in cabin or cockpit is a hand to mouth affair and the cocktail stick reigns supreme for such occasions.

A selection of sandwiches piled four deep and sliced downwards to produce layered cubes, which can then be stuck through with sticks, will make for ease of handling while eating in close company. Prepare chunks of chopped ham, chicken breast, pork luncheon meat, smoked sausage and bacon grill. Purchase from the local market olives, green and black, avocado pear, gherkins, cucumber, small onions and local cheeses. Make ready slices or cubes of bananas, pineapples, peaches, apricots, plums and apples. All these may be spiked on cocktail sticks in an infinite and attractive permutation of colour and taste. Since the skipper may throw the party at short notice, put cocktail sticks on the stores list.

As an alternative to the stick method of preparation, the smorgasbord technique is another simple way of serving a large variety of attractive snacks. Toasts or biscottes (twice baked bread slices), rye crispbreads, crackers or wafers are the usual types of base upon which to spread pâté, pastes, diced salads and savory mixes. A coating of butter or margarine on the base before the addition of the spread will waterproof and preserve the crispness of the snack. The snacks may all be prepared quickly from canned ingredients or cold left-overs. Some suggestions:

1. Cream cheese with grated orange peel.
2. Herring soft roes, bread crumbs, anchovy sauce and mixed herbs stirred to a paste.
3. Scrambled egg, cream and curry powder mixed.
4. A mixture of pilchards, French mustard and sweet chutney.
5. A mixed salad finely chopped and mixed with a cream mayonnaise.

Any one of the sandwich fillings in the recipe section on p. 63 will make an attractive open sandwich. All spreads may be decorated with olives, sliced cucumber, chopped radish, sliced red pepper or beetroot.

It is certain that every area in which it is possible to cruise will have its own delicacy peculiar to the locality. The least likely places often produce the most unusual and exciting novelties. Even the Pool of London can introduce newcomers to the delights of the cockneys' jellied eels. A visit to the market nearest the anchorage will enable the tastes of the natives to be served, in waxed paper cups, for the enjoyment of the guests aboard. According to the sea board such specialties will range from clams and crayfish of Key West to Thamesmouth cockles, from Greek sea urchin to Tahitian raw fish. The locality should provide the pleasurable element of surprise for the party.

Disposable tableware

Few small boats carry the crockery or the cutlery to serve a group which seems to multiply so rapidly once a social gathering aboard is underway. It is much easier, quicker and more efficient if paper plates, waxed paper cake cups and expendable plastic cutlery is used for parties. Packaged, such articles occupy little space and a quantity may be stowed easily at fitting out, they will not be needed every day. Their consumable nature is their greatest asset and the waxed paper bowls are just the right size for the service of the specialties among the snacks. Equally essential are the paper serviettes and paper towels so that hands and the immediate surroundings may be kept clean in what can easily and speedily become a messy situation.

Whilst enjoying the prospect of throwing away the dishes and cutlery rather than washing them, it is as well to keep a firm grip on the disposition of the resultant gash and garbage. A shipboard party can easily leave an indelible mark among the detritus of the tide line ashore. Gash bags and ashtrays must be readily available and their location made known with the first drink. No entertainment should advertise its programme with a down-tide slick of sticks, corks, paper and cellophane wrappers. Even the gulls from long apprenticeship to public ferries, disparage this indelible trade mark of anti-social behaviour and lack of litter discipline.

Glasses

In the name of stability, heavy based tumbler-type glasses, not necessarily of large tumbler size, are advisable for boat use. Stemmed glasses with their inbuilt fragility can so often result in the embarrassment of breakage. Plastic 'glasses' are unbreakable, an advantage, but quickly warm up in the hand, a disadvantage, and do not sparkle as appetisingly as do glasses. Paper cups and mugs are not a success with alcoholic drinks for it is all too easy to squeeze one's Scotch and slop the measure.

The guests do the talking

Jollification will be the merrier and entertainment the greater if the guests do the talking. Cockpits and cabins, especially in craft anchored offshore, can become prison cells, in which a captive audience endure the monopolistic verbal onslaught from the gaoler, their host. The variety of talk both in quality and quantity which results from the occasional prodding from the host can send the assembled group of strangers away as friends, even if only for the day. Cruising is made up of such chance encounters, and the most memorable of these are strung, like pearls, along the thread of memory in the log book. Above all it should never be assumed that the size of the craft or the burgee it flies at the masthead are in any way a measure or even indication of the owner's conviviality. So the haphazard meeting and chance conversation may reveal a wealth of experience, of wit and a vast knowledge of a common interest concealed behind the unprepossessing appearance of skipper, crew and craft.

Speeding the parting guest

Finally perhaps it is more difficult to bring a social gathering to an end than to warm its beginning. The visitors' book is a valued adjunct to the yacht's entertainment equipment. Casually produced with the invitation to sign up before leaving, this is the universally recognised signal to shove off. It is also a constant source of joy in recollection.

No host skipper should ever leave any of the guests at risk on their return journey to their respective craft. Conviviality is a heady wine, instability is its concomitant and drowning is a drastic method of diluting one's drink. A sober dinghy watch must be detailed to be available if any guest is likely to be a hazard when bunkward bound across water. Charon, the ferryman of the River Styx in Hades, is waiting and willing to stand in, if this courtesy is not observed.

Lamb kebabs – a famous dish from Turkey, delicious and easy to cook.

1 lb lamb, in cubes, 2 green peppers, caps and seeds removed, 2 tomatoes, 2 small onions, 2 courgettes, 2 mushrooms – sliced.

The marinade.
3 tablespoons olive oil, 2 tablespoons sherry, 1 clove garlic, finely chopped, 1 small onion, finely chopped, 1 tablespoon parsley, chopped, 1 teaspoon oregano, a dash of salt and pepper.

Use 4 long skewers.

Combine the marinade ingredients in a bowl. Cut the meat into $1\frac{1}{2}$ in. cubes and immerse in the marinade. Cover the bowl and allow meat to stand for some hours (use a sealed plastic box if cruising, the motion will mix the meat). Cut vegetables in pieces and skewer meat alternately with pepper, onion, mushrooms, courgettes, put tomato halves at the end of the skewer. Brush with the marinade and grill turning frequently. Serve with rice pilaff.

Section 9

FIRST AID AND SEA SICKNESS

First principles

Injury and illness in any member of a boat's crew away from land demands the only assistance there can be – first aid. That this will only be aid and not medical care should be anticipated. Any accident or sickness other than minor cuts and bruises, the common ailments such as colds or constipation and the occupational hazard of sickness, should be taken seriously.

If the health and condition of any crew member is suspect, don't hang about. Make for the nearest port as soon as possible, for weather can change rapidly for the worse. Delay may compel the acceptance of risks which good seamanship would seek to avoid. First aid methods have four objectives:

1. The restoration and/or maintenance of breathing and heart beat.
2. The control of bleeding.
3. The prevention of further injury or infection.
4. The treatment of shock.

The first two aims are covered by mouth-to-mouth resuscitation and heart massage. These methods should be known to all who sail, and any 'man overboard' practice should include a rehearsal of both. *First Aid for Yachtsmen*, also published by Adlard Coles Ltd, or a reliable first aid manual appears as number one item in the first aid kit, and the method of applying both these vital aids will be shown therein. The skipper and the cook should have the 'know how' without the book, since both operations need a relay of practitioners. The control of bleeding also requires some knowledge, and speed is of the essence in practice. Certainty of the location of the principal pressure points for main arterial bleeding in legs, arms and neck should be common knowledge to a crew. The prevention of further injury and infection requires the practice of that old first aid adage 'Eyes first and most, fingers last and least.' An unhurried thorough examination of the injury carried out with confidence, gentleness and diligence is the proper approach to the emergency.

The fourth aim covers the commonest result of accident, the physical state known as shock. Shock is the illness of injury. It may be caused by loss of blood, by cold, by emotional collapse. Shock can result from falling overboard or from the intense pain of jamming a finger in the mainsheet runner. It often arises from fear or seasickness. The signs of shock are a low temperature, rapid respiration, a pulse rate of 100 +, a pale appearance, nausea and cold perspiration. The patient should lie down, the feet should be raised and the head lowered to create a difference in level of some 1–2 ft. Then, as comfort, provide warmth, blankets and a hot water bottle. Give warm drink with care as this may cause vomiting. Alcohol is not advised because by dilating the capillaries, it induces chill. Even mild shock, a common condition after an injury, can considerably reduce the efficiency and capacity of a crew member, more so sometimes than the injury which causes the condition.

Cuts and grazes

Minor cuts and grazes are almost a daily ration for crew members afloat. So common are the scratches and nips that they have been described by one lone sailor as 'boat bites'. Unless of a major nature, accompanied by arterial bleeding, cuts and grazes should be treated as a breach in the armour of the skin, an entry for invading infection. The wound should be washed with a surgical antiseptic and cleaned thoroughly. It should then be covered with a sterile dressing. Prepared sterile pads and tubular or elastic netted dressings are admirable since they can be pulled over awkward contours and are self-fastening. If bandage is used, a Sellotape binding is a quicker, more effective fastening than knots or safety pins. The dressed wound should be protected if possible with a waterproof cover, a finger or thumbstall or a plastic bag for feet.

Severe wounds with heavy arterial bleeding need urgent medical attention and skill. Large absorbant sterile pads and pressure at the correct spot are immediate requirements. A tourniquet is not recommended, but if one is applied the time of application should be noted, for the blood flow must not be cut off for too long a period at a time – at most 15 minutes. These preliminary steps together with treatment for shock are all that first aid can achieve. Speed towards assistance is then of vital importance. After some 12 hours elapsed time deep wounds cannot be stitched.

Bruises and contusions

These painful results of a blow are difficult injuries to treat with first aid. A heavy blow can cause concealed bone damage, not easily recognised by emergency amateur diagnosis. The old-fashioned tincture of arnica, so strongly advised by the last homoeopathic generation is still a good treatment. It has been replaced by a number of ointments and sprays all of which do the same job. The bruised tissues and contused blood capillaries have to be slowly and naturally repaired. Again comfort, relief in some measure of the pain of the injury, is all that can be achieved by first aid. Bathed with cold water, painted with tincture of arnica and protected and supported by a dressing of elastic crêpe bandage, the worst of the hurt will subside. Watch carefully for swelling of the area and for painful reactions in movement of the limb which may indicate bone damage.

Burns and scalds

Burns and scalds are always to be taken seriously both as injuries liable to infection and as causes of shock. The first step must be to remove from the area any restricting clothing, watches or jewellery. The next immediate stage of treatment is to remove the residual heat from the burn area. Cooled by the application of pads of wadding continuously soaked in cold water or, if possible, plunged into frequently renewed cold water, this treatment should be continued for 10 to 15 minutes. The burn area should be dried carefully and covered with a sterile dressing. No ointment or salves should be used. If the burn area is severely injured do not attempt to remove charred clothing or skin. Apply the cold treatment using a saline solution and cover carefully with a sterile dressing. A burn of this nature is a very serious injury and needs professional attention as soon as possible. Such burns also cause severe shock. Blisters resulting from burns or scalds should never be pricked or burst. Kept covered with a dressing, the area must be left to dry out naturally.

The self-inflicted wounds. Sunburn and constipation

Sunburn can only occur as a result of negligence. The much-admired deep tan, the desire of both male and female sunstarved white skins, cannot be achieved naturally in the space of a few hours. The radiation which encourages the skin to produce the pigmentation protection and the vitamin D which goes with it, is a milder variety of the atomic bomb bombardment. Common sense dictates that lacking the warning of chill on the skin, exposure can continue almost unnoticed if the individual is busily occupied. The process of acquiring a suntan must be a series of progressively extended exposure periods, over several days, if starting from scratch. During these periods various lotions will baste the meat to prevent burning. Over exposure is stupid, and, in a team sailing a cruiser, an act of sabotage. The first aid procedure should commence before the lobster-red flush appears. The lily-white figure should be watched for the first few days and should be ordered to use barrier creams and suntan lotions, or to cover up frequently. If, however, caution has been thrown to the winds and vast areas of irradiated cooked flesh result, the application of calamine lotion will alleviate some of the pain. As with all burns, blisters should not be burst, and peeling skin should not be pulled away. Infection and a second dose of sun radiation can cause serious physical conditions if the burned area is not covered and treated carefully.

Constipation

The bunged up condition of the bowel which is a plague to those who have ignored the requests of nature, because they were busy or preoccupied or just lazy, is a frequent cause for malaise afloat. The obvious treatment is a dose of any one of a number of alimentary explosives. This is, for a period, as uncomfortable as the condition being treated and reduces the effectiveness of the individual in the meantime. Better by far is the prevention of the condition, caused simply by an accumulation of waste product. A regular issue every other day at breakfast time of a measure of roughage, e.g. bran, together with a daily portion of fresh fruit in the diet, will usually prevent constipation developing. It is, however, a self-inflicted complaint and all the treatment up to and including dynamite will be of little avail if nature's message for evacuation is ignored.

Seasickness

There is no shame in the condition which Nelson suffered for the first day or so every time he went to sea. Caused by the psychological effect of conflicting messages from the two senses of seeing and balance, there is no cure nor prevention which can guarantee to be successful and have no side effects. The author was last seasick at the age of five and the cure which has lasted several thousand miles of sailing was only effective because of the permanence of its traumatic effect.

Every time I was sick, the steward appointed to look after me on a voyage to the Mediterranean shovelled great spoonfuls of mashed potatoes and lamb stew into my quivering mouth. No sooner was it down than it was up again. In recollection I cannot be certain that the supply which lasted for two days was fresh on every occasion. I have never been seasick since at sea. I am seasick immediately if I am presented with mashed potatoes or smell lamb stew – even in a hotel restaurant. The moral of the tale is that what works for one does not necessarily help another, and circumstances differ. Seasick tablets are readily available. Experiment on yourself and the best of luck. If always seasick and severely so, stay ashore for you will be useless aboard and only make a mess withal. The quickly-over bout of sickness which some crews suffer at the start of a season is little cause for treatment medically. 'Keep going' should be the motto. Stay in the open air, find a job to do, move about. The best therapy for seasickness is operational.

Sufferers from seasickness should not be allowed to vomit over the side. It is a dangerous situation for one already less than in full possession of his senses and can easily lead to falling overboard. A seasick individual does not always differentiate between windward and leeward, and so shares his distress with the other occupants of the cockpit. Sickness of any kind is a dehydrating process and water to sip should be at hand for the sufferer while the condition lasts.

The first aid kit

The kit should be kept in a box, should be readily accessible and should have a sling attachment for transportation so that two hands remain free while moving with the kit to the scene of the injury. It should include the following items:

A first aid manual.
Waterproof adhesive first aid dressings in several sizes and shapes.
Bandages with sealed sterile dressings attached in several sizes.
Surgical lint.
Cotton wool.
2 in. adhesive strip.
3-in.-wide crêpe bandage.
A roll of 2 in. Sellotape.
1 pkt. (50) safety pins.
A triangular bandage or sling.
Surgiflex dressings (surgical expanding net).
Tubinette dressings (tubular surgical expanding bandage).
Melolin antiseptic wound dressings (large size).
2 fingerstalls, 2 thumbstalls (waterproof).
1 pair scissors.
1 pair tweezers.
1 clinical thermometer.
1 bottle surgical antiseptic.
1 bottle calamine lotion.
1 bottle eye lotion (Optrex).
1 eye bath.
1 tube lip salve.
1 bottle suntan lotion.
100 aspirin, Anadin or Disprin tablets.
Laxative tablets.
1 hot water bottle.
1 small torch.
1 bottle surgical spirit.

To the contents of any first aid kit aboard should be added those pieces of sailing equipment which can be modified in use to serve the emergency of injury. Sail battens will form effective splints, sail tiers make tourniquet straps, ensigns and teatowels convert to slings, table salt makes an antiseptic solution. Ingenuity and cool headed improvisation are hall marks of good first aid practice afloat.

Aubergines with ham stuffing

4 aubergines
¼ pint olive oil
6 oz. ham, diced
1 tablespoon flour
¼ pint milk
1 tablespoon lemon juice
Dried breadcrumbs
1 oz. butter

Cut the aubergines in half lengthwise and dig out the pulp to form a shell, leaving the skin unbroken. Dice the pulp. Heat the oil moderately in a pan and sauté the aubergine shells for 10 minutes, turning carefully. Remove and drain on paper towels. In the same oil sauté the diced aubergine pulp. To this add the diced ham, sprinkle with flour and stir with a spoon until the ham is brown. Add milk and lemon juice to the pan. Stir and cook until the mixture is thick. Fill the aubergine shells with the mix and sprinkle with breadcrumbs and dot with butter. Grill to brown and serve.

Part II

FEEDING THE CREW

The recipes

All the recipes given have been tried successfully aboard *Mistress Softly*, a 24 ft. auxiliary sloop, using a stove with two burners and a grill, and the utensils and tools listed in the Appendices.

The restrictions on fresh ingredients have been kept in mind but a limited number using fresh meat and fresh fish have been included. Fresh fish should not present any difficulty afloat. The fresh meats used are the common cuts of popular meat easily purchased in any market. Fresh vegetables used are those with a storage life of several days. Cream used is always longlife cream in cartons. Eggs are always those preserved by greasing. These kept fresh for 10 weeks in the Mediterranean in summer.

Section 10

Sandwiches, starters and savouries

The ubiquitous sandwich, which enabled the noble lord after whom it is named to gamble with time in hand, continues all these years later to give the sailing man sustenance whilst cheating wind and tide. A pack of sandwiches and flasks filled with hot soup or cold orange juice represent the emergency feeding arrangements for most small boats on passage. The clever ship's cook will have at his fingertips all the many ingredients which will give each day's sandwiches a difference. The varieties listed below will enable you to sail for almost a month without repetition, and all good cooks will have their own specialties not included in this list to prepare a few more rounds before having to start at the beginning again.

Bread is, of course, a problem. Rolls may be baked in a pressure cooker, and loaves may be revived by cutting the loaf in half longways, damping the cut surfaces with a little milk and putting the two halves together again. The loaf is then wrapped in metal foil sheet, sealed and placed in the pressure cooker, with half a pint of water. When pressure has been raised, cook for 5 minutes only. Then remove. However, when sandwiches are made with fresh baked bread they are consumed at twice the rate of those made with stale bread.

27 varieties of sandwich fillings

1. Grated cheese and mango chutney.
2. Cream cheese mixed with chopped chives or chopped spring onion tops.
3. Cheese mixed with a teaspoonful of grated onion and cream, or the top of the milk.
4. Lancashire cheese (red) and raisins.
5. Cream cheese and lemon curd.
6. Sliced corned beef and chopped onion.
7. Sliced chopped ham and pork with thin sliced tomato.
8. Flaked tuna fish and sliced hard boiled egg.
9. Mashed sardines and thin peeled lemon slices.
10. Mashed corned beef and sliced gherkin.
11. Cheese spread and sliced stoned green olives.
12. Sliced chopped ham and pork with chopped pickled walnuts.
13. Cheese spread with chopped green pepper.
14. Pink salmon mashed with diced cucumber and mayonnaise.
15. Sliced corned beef with shredded cabbage heart and mayonnaise.
16. Sardines with lettuce and thin sliced peeled tomato.
17. Shrimps or prawns chopped with diced cucumber and mayonnaise.
18. Cream cheese mixed with grated orange peel.
19. Hard boiled egg chopped with parsley and mixed with mayonnaise.
20. Diced cold chicken and crumbled crisp fried bacon.
21. Dressed crab and grated cucumber mixed with mayonnaise.
22. Corned beef mashed with chopped chives and tomato ketchup.
23. Cold scrambled egg and chopped pimento (canned pimentos may be used).
24. Cottage cheese mixed with grated carrot and chopped gherkin.
25. Liver sausage and chopped tomato.
26. Salami sausage, chopped cabbage heart and mayonnaise.
27. Chopped fried bacon, scrambled egg and mushrooms.

To these may be added the lighter sandwiches filled with any of the large variety of prepared fish, meat and savoury spreads in jars, tubes and tins available everywhere. Remember also that jam and cream, or honey and cream or banana and cream give a tasty second course to a sandwich meal.

Starters

Afloat, in Nelson's day, the starter was a cane wielded by the junior officers or gunners' mates to urge the crew to greater efforts in the performance of their duties. Compared with the practice of lashing with a cat-o'-nine-tails, the culprit strapped to a grating, the use of a starter was a mere rebuke. In the world of the galley, the starter is still an inducement, a signal to the glands to begin salivation in preparation for the courses to follow. Easily prepared, speedily presented, appetising in appearance and readily consumed by hand to mouth, starters are also a gentle reminder to the crew that the chores of meal preparations are to be shared. It is the cook's method of encouraging co-operation. Sweet or savoury, raw or cooked, they should be easily handled, should be accompanied by the first drink of the meal, and paper handkerchiefs or tissues should be provided.

Salami cocktail tidbits

1 avocado pear
mayonnaise
lemon juice
thinly sliced salami sausage

Peel and stone the avocado, cut into small cubes and dip into the lemon juice/mayonnaise mix. Serve spiked on cocktail sticks with rolled slices of salami sausage.

Sweety tidbits

Crispbreads spread with cream cheese topped with morella cherry jam.

Shrimp crush

Crispbreads topped with canned shrimps mixed with mayonnaise, garnish each slice with ½ a ring of lemon.

Crunchy raisins

Crispbread spread with peanut butter mixed with chopped stoned raisins.

Pineapple toppers

Buttered wholemeal bread slice, spread with cress and piled with a mix of cottage cheese and chopped spring onion tops. Cut each slice into six squares and top each square with a pineapple cube.

Pâté snippets

Crispbread spread with pâté de foie and topped with stoned green olives.

Canapé spread

Blend tinned herring roes with a teaspoon of capers and mayonnaise. Spread the mix on squares of French toast.

Meaty bites

Mix minced corned beef with a little condensed oxtail soup to make a spread. Cover crispbread or French toast squares with the mixture and garnish with radish slices.

Crab and cheese florets

Mix 1 can of crab meat with 4 oz. cottage cheese, 3 chopped gherkins and a dash of chilli sauce. Blend to a creamy mixture with mayonnaise. Dunk raw cauliflower florets on cocktail sticks in the mixture. Serve.

Blue cheese spread

Mash 4 oz. blue cheese with 3 tablespoons of butter. Season with pepper and beat in a tablespoon of brandy. Allow to stand for 1 hour. Spread the mixture on fingers of French toast.

Stilton cheese dip

Crumble 2 oz. Stilton cheese into lightly whipped cream. Add crumbled crisp-fried bacon and mix. Spread on crispbread, garnish with grated carrot.

Savouries

Cooked savoury dishes may be served both as starters or as a conclusion to a meal. The following six recipes could be used for either purpose. If serving them at the end of a meal, prepare all the ingredients beforehand so that the dish requires only the minimum of attention and time before serving.

Avocado grill

4 oz. bacon
6 oz. grated cheese
1 avocado pear, stoned, peeled and thinly sliced. Sprinkle with lemon juice to prevent browning
4 soft rolls, split and buttered, toasted
Mustard to taste

Cut the bacon into strips, fry until crisp and keep hot. Place the avocado slices on the toasted roll halves and brush lightly with mustard. Sprinkle grated cheese on top making sure the avocado slices are covered. Grill until the cheese melts. Top with crisp bacon strips.

Fried herring roes

1 can (4 oz.) soft herring roes
Parsley flour
2 rounds hot buttered toast
3 anchovy fillets
Cooking oil

Drain the herring roes and coat them by shaking in a paper bag of seasoned flour. Fry roes for a few minutes in hot oil. To 3 tablespoons butter add 3 fillets of anchovies, pound together to make a paste. Spread this paste on the hot buttered toast. Add the fried roes and serve.

Kipper toasts

1 can kipper fillets
1 oz. butter
3 slices bread
3 fillets anchovies
1 tablespoon milk

Cook the kippers according to directions on the can. Pound together butter and anchovies, add milk. Flake the cooked kipper fillets into the mix and beat. Spread the mixture on fingers of toast and serve hot, at once.

Huelvos cocotte à la Castelanna

3 eggs
½ onion chopped.
2 oz. minced beef
1 tablespoon grated cheese
Olive oil
½ pint béchamel sauce (see Sauces)

Fry the chopped onion until clear, add the mince and fry until brown. Line small oven-proof glass bowls (dessert bowls) with a drop of oil and a portion of the fried mince. On to this cooked meat, break an egg. Put bowls under grill until egg white sets, add the béchamel sauce. Sprinkle grated cheese on the sauce and return to the grill for a couple of minutes. Serve immediately.

Egg and mushroom savoury

4–6 hard boiled eggs
Chopped parsley
Croutons
3 oz. grated cheddar cheese
1 can cream of mushroom sauce

Prepare two cupfuls of croutons. Croutons are small cubes of bread fried golden brown in butter. A supply of these invaluable additions to dips and soups will keep for a few days in a screw-top container in the cool.

Slice the hard boiled eggs lengthways and place in a shallow oven-proof glass dish. Heat the soup and pour over the eggs. Sprinkle with grated cheese and brown under the grill. Garnish with croutons and chopped parsley. Serve immediately.

Scrambled eggs with shrimps

6 oz. can peeled shrimps
2 oz. butter
5 tablespoons milk
8 eggs
1 tablespoon chopped parsley
Salt and pepper to taste

Drain shrimps and rinse well in cold water. Reserve some shrimps as garnish, chop the remainder coarsely. Place milk and butter in a frying pan and heat gently until the butter melts. Break eggs into a basin, beat lightly, stirring in shrimps, parsley, salt and pepper. Pour egg mixture on to the milk and butter and cook, gently stirring all the time as mixture thickens, but not set in a rubbery mess. Transfer to a warmed dish and garnish with the remaining shrimps. Serve with buttered toasts.

Section 11

Herbs, spices, seasonings and aromas

One of the measures which separates the mere carbonisers of food from the ship's master cook is skill in seasoning. This subtle art can be traced back beyond Macbeth's three witches, beyond Cleopatra's pearled vinegar salad dressing to the love potions of Eros lost in ancient time. It was long believed by the vitalising witch doctors of the far east that passion and virility could result from dishes and beverages concocted from herbs and mysterious brews of spices. It is true that surprising results have accrued from the use of chilli pepper, ginseng root, cardamon and cinnamon. It is also as well to be forewarned of the power of this herbal dynamite, for the aim is a smile on the face, not tears in the eyes, as swallow follows swallow.

It all begins, as does so much of the joy of sailing, with a cautious approach. Just a pinch in the right place is frequently all that is needed. So, if you are still with it, a prepared chart is before you – use it and prosper. Remember that the essence of dried herbs is much more concentrated than the fresh material, so that one teaspoonful of dried may be the equivalent of a tablespoon of fresh. The volatile oils which are the essence of herbs and spices are quickly dispersed and lost if the cooking process is long or the temperature high. Except in closed pots, stews and braises, the herbs and spices should be added during the last stage of cooking. Curry powder is greatly improved in taste if slowly heated in a little melted butter immediately before use. Since the aromas of herbs and spices are an additional dividend to the meal, cover the dishes before serving. The appetising smell suddenly pervading the cabin as the dish is uncovered can divert the crew prematurely from the more important tasks of working the ship.

Whereas fresh herbs, with the possible exception of mint or parsley, are a rarity nowadays, dried herbs and spices can be bought at any time. The village markets of Mexico, Spain and France may still sell dried bunches of tarragon, fennel and rosemary, but a collection of dried varieties stored in small jars screwed tight and stowed securely after use, is the easiest way to keep a store of what the chefs call 'this and that'.

Below is a simple representative selection with some suggested uses.

Herbs

Basil – A mild though pungent herb. Use sparingly while cooking tomatoes, aubergines, in salad and grilled lamb chops.

Bay leaf – Mildly aromatic, very pungent, use sparingly, one leaf at a time, in stews, court bouillon and marinades. Remove from dish before serving.

Chervil – Mild pleasant savour in all green salads.

Chives – A light onion taste used to season all salads, cheese and egg dishes.

Dill – A mild pleasant herb. Add to taste in dishes of tunny fish, salmon, cucumbers and potatoes.

Fennel *(seeds)* – A mild aromatic herb especially suited to fish.

Marjoram – Pungent and slightly bitter, use sparingly in sea-food cooking, rub over pork and lamb, add to meat stuffings.

Mint – A fresh mild herb, added according to taste to new potatoes, peas and roasted lamb.

Oregano – Adds a strong distinctive aromatic taste to shell fish. Use with care in sauces for meat, a must in all pizza dishes.

Parsley – A mild fresh herb. Can be used in quantity with fish, in white sauces and in omelettes.

Rosemary – A distinctive, aromatic sweet flavoured herb, should be used sparingly with pork, lamb, fish, especially trout, and in marinades for meat and fish.

Sage – A soft aromatic herb. Use with discretion in stuffings, with onions and in baked fish dishes.

Tarragon – Has a taste reminiscent of aniseed. Add sparingly and judiciously to salads and in meat and fish marinades. A little improves vinegar a lot.

Thyme – Use this pungent aromatic herb with care. Improves carrot, aubergine and celery dishes, gives an added zest to eggs, liver and bacon. Is excellent with grilled fresh salmon.

Spices

Cinnamon – A very aromatic sweet spice. Used in baked sweet dishes, baked apples, is a lovely addition to a wine cup, and a distinctive ingredient in mulled ale.

Cloves – A warm, aromatic pungent spice which must be used sparingly – one clove at a time. Adds a new dimension to grilled gammon or to apple pie.

Curry Powder – A mixture of spices, it is a culinary blow lamp. It must be used with great discretion and very much according to taste. Too much and no taste is left for hours. Use in dishes of curried eggs, fish, meats and shell fish and in rice cooking.

Ginger – Hot! But a sweet clean taste. Adjust to personal requirements with melon, apple pie and fruit and in sweet sour sauces.

Nutmeg – A mild warm enriching spice used with carrots, spinach, cream cheese, game marinades and baked desserts.

Pepper – White – The mildest of the family.

Black – Use fresh from the hand mill if possible, when it will be deliciously scented. Used sparingly in marinades and with grilled meat and herrings.

Cayenne – A very hot biting aromatic pepper

used cautiously in hot stews and Caribbean dishes.

Chilli – Very, very hot. Let not the hand shake in use. For pizzas and meat marinades. Remember that water will not put out the fire once started!

Saffron – The most expensive of the spices. An exotic aroma, it should be used sparingly. For the best results, wrap a few stamens in a fold of foil and warm this before use. Crumble when using with rice as a colouring, and as an additive to fish soups, bouillebaise or bacalao vizcama.

Turmeric – Very mild, it is used as a cheaper method of colouring in place of saffron. Add just a shake to mayonnaise and in Moroccan lamb dishes. It is a constituent of most curry powders.

Garlic

It has been said that real happiness can only be found where garlic enters cooking. Certainly this small corm carries with it the potential to knit companionship closer or to separate friends for ever. Certainly garlic features in many of the greatest dishes of the Mediterranean countries and is inevitably associated with blue skies, a wine-dark sea and wine in abundance.

Why not try it with a joint of lamb. Into knife slits in the meat insert some 10–15 thin slices of garlic corm, roast and serve to your friends. This is seasoning for the gods.

Section 12

Sauces for courses

The sailor was ever supposed to be a saucy fellow, the adjective referring of course to his general enthusiasm, which ashore lit up his personality. The word could just as well have been derived from the necessity to use a sauce in his diet of salt pork and ancient beef in brine to cover up the taste and mask the repulsive appearance of what passed for ship's food in the days of hemp and canvas. It is still true today that a sauce may help to cover up a less than perfect preparation or disguise the somewhat elderly constituents of the dish. Currying, for example, was long considered to be only one stage away from burial in hot climates. But the principal purpose of a sauce is to accent or enhance the relish of a prepared dish. The list of sauces is endless for their cooking has long been regarded as a chef's very own personal alchemy. Here are a few well tried elixirs to jog the flagging palate. Nothing can be expected to conceal bad cooking.

Béchamel sauce

2 tablespoons butter
2 tablespoons flour
1 cup milk
Salt and pepper to taste

Melt the butter in a small pan and when melted stir in the flour, mixing well. Add the milk, salt and pepper gradually, stirring constantly. Cook for 5 minutes and serve.

The butter and flour mix is called a roux. If the butter is too hot when the flour is added, or if the flour is left to cook too long in the butter alone, the result will be a greyish brown mess. The flour should absorb all the butter and at that moment the liquid, in this case the cold milk, is added. Only cold liquids can be added to a hot roux, otherwise curdling results. The cooked roux of butter and flour will keep for 24 hours and can then be used cold to prepare a sauce. The cold roux must be cooked with a hot liquid such as milk or a bouillon, stirring all the time.

From this basic béchamel sauce further sauces may be prepared, thus.

(a) Stir into the béchamel sauce ¼ lb of grated Gruyère cheese. This will make sauce mornay for fish.

(b) Add to the béchamel sauce a small can of tomato purée. This will give a sauce aurore for poached eggs.

(c) The addition of the juice of a lemon, a glass of white wine and (off the flame so that it does not curdle) the beaten yolks of two eggs makes sauce poulette to serve with chicken.

(d) Add 1 tablespoon of lemon juice and 2 tablespoons of prepared mustard. Stir and the result will be sauce moutarde, a fine accompaniment to grilled mackerel.

Sauce bordelaise

¼ cup minced onions
1 teaspoon minced garlic
½ cup butter
1 tablespoon parsley
1 tablespoon lemon juice
¼ cup flour
1 teaspoon tomato purée
¼ teaspoon thyme
1 bay leaf
1 cup stock (Beef extract or cube)

Sauté the onions and garlic in the butter for 5 minutes. As for a roux, stir in the flour and then add the stock, stirring all the time. Add the bay leaf and cook for 5 minutes. Remove the bay leaf and add the rest of the ingredients stirring all the while. Allow to simmer for 5 minutes. If the sauce becomes too thick add a little more stock. Sauce bordelaise is a fine additive for grilled or roasted meats. If a chicken extract or bouillon cube is substituted for the beef stock, a sauce for addition to poached fish results.

Sweet sour lemon sauce

2 tablespoons olive oil
1 tablespoon onion flakes
⅓ cup brown sugar
1 tablespoon cornflour
½ teaspoon dry mustard
½ cup lemon juice
1 tablespoon soy sauce
½ teaspoon garlic salt

Soak the onion flakes and garlic salt in the oil. Mix together the mustard, sugar and cornflour, stir in the soy sauce and lemon juice to make a smooth mixture. At this point add the onion, garlic salt and oil mix. Cook, stirring until thick, and continue cooking for 5 minutes. This is a delicious sauce for any sea food.

The sauces given will serve for a large variety of recipes and menus. The only difficulty lies in the quality of the initial roux. If this is overdone, a discoloured separated mess results; if underdone a good wall covering paste results. Experience will get it right and the perfection will be greeted with acclaim. You may if rushed, tired, overworked, lazy or frightened, take an easy way out. There are a vast range of soup mixes which, if concentrated by a reduction in the liquid quantity used, will serve as sauces. Canned concentrated soups are even lazier, as there is no need to boil water or stir!

Section 13

Soups

In these days of instant soups from tins or cans or from dehydrated constituents in packets and compressed cubes, it would seem superfluous to concern the ship's cook with soup. Add water, bring to the boil, simmer and serve, dismisses soup in as many minutes as it takes to read. But the wonders of modern physics and chemistry cannot prevent dehydration and processing, synthesis and freeze drying from taking the guts out of soup. The great part of the population of the world has subsisted for centuries on a diet of soup and bread so it little behoves the owner of some 30 ft. of fibreglass marine engineering to scoff at the pot.

Some recipes for real soup are given here. The pressure cooker will shorten the preparation time, preserve the product and permutate the properties of the remaining contents of one soup cooker when added to the next. But first the most famous soup in the world – a meal in itself from Les Halles, the market of Paris.

French onion soup

5 large onions
1½ oz. butter
4 teaspoons flour
¼ pint dry white wine
8 thin slices white bread
5 oz. Gruyère cheese
Salt and pepper

Peel and slice the onions thinly. Melt the butter in the pan. Add the onions and cook until golden. Sprinkle in the flour and cook as a roux. Add the wine and 1 pint boiling water. Dry the bread under the grill but do not brown. Slice the cheese very thin. Put into a large warmed oven-proof glass bowl (with lid), alternate layers of bread and cheese slices. Over this pour the hot soup. Place the bowl on two asbestos mats on the stove and cook for 20 minutes.

Lentil and tomato soup

This is the soup the Roman legions marched on.

10 oz. lentils
1 large can tomatoes
2 pints beef stock
¼ bottle dry white wine
1 bunch celery, chopped, leaves as well
1 large onion, sliced
1 tablespoon parsley
1 tablespoon butter
2 cups rice
1 clove garlic finely chopped

Chop the onion and fry with the garlic in the butter until golden. Chop the celery with the leaves. Put rice, lentils, celery, cooked onion and tomatoes into the pressure cooker. Add wine, stock and parsley. Bring to pressure and cook for 20 minutes. Serve with croutons.

An interesting exercise is to make up a lentil soup preparation according to directions on the packet or can. Serve at the same time as the recipe above, and compare.

Borsch, a beetroot soup

1 lb diced cooked beetroot
½ red cabbage, coarsely shredded
2 potatoes, diced
2 onions, chopped
½ lb mushrooms, sliced
½ pint sour cream
1½ pt. beef stock
2 carrots, sliced
2 leeks, sliced

1 bay leaf
6 peppercorns
1 teaspoon garlic salt
1 tablespoon parsley

Put all of the ingredients except the sour cream in the pressure cooker, adding seasoning and stock. Bring to pressure and cook for 20 minutes. Reduce pressure and strain contents through a sieve into an oven-proof bowl. Add sour cream, stir and keep warm on the stove. Serve with a tot of vodka per portion. This is optional but not superfluous.

If one half of Europe lived on lentil and onion soup, the rest lived equally well on Borsch, which can be eaten hot or cold according to détente.

Hot soup, in Thermos flasks, is the mainstay to long night watches. Keep a pressure cooker of soup going while passage making. It is as necessary as an inflatable life raft and the equal of an extra crew member.

Section 14

Salads

At the mention of salad many individuals retort 'rabbit food!' Well, maybe it is, but have you ever seen an overweight undersexed rabbit?

Practically any vegetable and fruit will serve as a constituent for a salad, so salad making is a vast field for the cook's ingenuity. Certain basic principles apply, however, whatever the salad. First both vegetables and fruit should be fresh, the salad dressing should be carefully prepared to complement the salad, and the finished dish should look appetising and attractive. With these provisos a salad can be served to accompany cold cuts or as a highlight for lunch. A salad can complement the main dish for an evening meal or serve as an appetiser to start the meal, and salads consisting largely of fruit can be an attractive finish to the meal.

Afloat where the term 'fresh' presents certain problems of availability, it is well to remember that items such as cress, cabbage, cauliflower, cucumber, peppers, celery, endive or chicory remain 'fresh' much longer than lettuce or watercress, both of which fade rapidly with storage. Lettuce especially requires tender handling and should be eaten within the day of purchase. A piece of coal may be an odd item to include in the ship's stores, but it will revitalise limp lettuce if put with it into a bowl of fresh water. Lettuce needs to be washed thoroughly in fresh water. Cold running water is a wasteful process afloat. If the lettuce has a heart do not separate the leaves but stand it upside down for 20 minutes after washing to drain. Finally, throw off any remaining moisture by shaking it gently in a salad basket (a collapsible type in wire mesh). If leaves have been torn off, they should also be drained in the same manner. Lettuce should never be cut or chopped, it should always be torn into pieces. The leaves bruise easily and as a result taste bitter if cut or chopped. Strictly speaking a green salad should consist of a single green vegetable served raw with a dressing. Its preparation outlines the basic procedure for any salad. Wash the green vegetable, lettuce, watercress, heart of cabbage, thoroughly in cold water, and shake very well. Take a clove of garlic and beat the corm with the handle of a knife. It will then peel easily. Grind the peeled clove of garlic, held between thumb and finger, into a teaspoon of salt in the bottom of the salad bowl. When half the garlic is consumed, discard the rest. Add the salad greens, torn if lettuce, shredded if cabbage, to the salad bowl and sprinkle with a little crushed or mixed herbs, tarragon, oregano, chives or mint. Sprinkle two tablespoons of olive oil over the greens and toss gently until all the leaves appear shiny with oil. Stir into the bowl two tablespoons of white wine vinegar. Toss once more and serve.

No salad is complete without its dressing and no one type will suit all salads. As an additive to the salad the dressing needs to accent the basic taste of the ingredients. Egg, fish or meat salads need a piquant mixture whilst salads containing fruit or cheese are best complemented with a creamy addition. Prepare the salad dressing at the last moment and add it to the dish just before serving. Practice is required to make just sufficient to coat the leaves and no more. The puddle of curdled liquid at the bottom of the bowl after the dish has been served is the measure of the need for further care and practice. Many of the herbs and spices which accompany cooked meat and fish will go well in the accompanying dressing. Thus, horseradish sauce added to the oil and vinegar will go well with salt beef salad. Parmesan cheese will give zest to a salad of hard boiled eggs. Making mayonnaise is a long, laborious and skilled process ashore. It needs more time and beating than meals afloat should take, and failure, an all too easy result, ends in an inedible, curdled mess. A bottle of prepared mayonnaise thinned with single cream is more certain of success and is usually popular.

All the salads and dressings which follow are easily prepared aboard. A visit to a market twice in seven days will enable the perishable items to be bought. Store celery, heart of cabbage, radishes, cooked beetroot, cucumber, peppers and root vegetables in nets in a cool, well-ventilated store – the loo?

In those boats which do not have a fridge or an ice-box, tomatoes should be kept in a plastic box next the hull below the water line. Tinned or canned vegetables, peas, beans, carrots, mixed vegetables, mushrooms and tomatoes can all be used, if drained, as additives to a core of fresh vegetables. New potatoes, if buttered after cooking, to be used in cold salads should be washed with hot water before being added to the dish – the butter and the salad dressing will disagree. Sir Francis Chichester's cress garden is an invaluable hint on how to keep a supply of fresh green-stuff on hand. Buy the cress, ready grown in plastic pots, store it in the side wall lockers, and air and water it sparingly (fresh water of course). It will last for several days in good condition, depending upon the greenness of the fingers. Lettuce is the most perishable of green vegetables. However, wherever shredded cabbage is mentioned in a salad recipe, lettuce could be substituted. Vegetable salads are a hearty healthy item in any meal and are a delicious addition afloat if the weather is warm and sunny. Most salads are easily transported, so prepare the dish, pack it in a plastic container and row the meal ashore to that little cove. The thought of the crowded cafés in the nearest holiday resort will be the finest aperitif ever tasted.

Orange and cucumber salad

4 Tangerine oranges or 2 large oranges or canned Mandarin orange slices, strained
1 small cucumber
½ head of cabbage
½ mild onion

Dressing

¼ pint salad oil
3 tablespoons white wine vinegar
¼ teaspoon chilli powder
Salt and pepper to taste

Peel oranges removing all pith, and slice, or cut orange segments in halves, slice onion and separate into thin rings. Chop cabbage heart fairly coarse and arrange in a salad bowl with cucumber slices and orange segments mixed. Top the salad with onion rings. Mix the dressing ingredients, thoroughly sprinkle over salad and serve.

Deep water salad

This is a salad which can be concocted from canned or dehydrated vegetables and it can be made in advance, an advantage for passage-making meals.

2 pkt. dehydrated mixed vegetables or 1 large can mixed vegetables
½ head cabbage, chopped (or a lettuce or watercress)
1 can asparagus tips
1 small onion, chopped
2 teaspoons vinegar
1 teaspoon dill
½ teaspoon castor sugar
¼ teaspoon salt
½ cup mayonnaise
1 tablespoon parsley

Cook the dehydrated vegetables according to directions and allow to cool. Or drain canned vegetables. Blend vegetables with onions and chopped cabbage (or lettuce or watercress) in salad bowl. Mix vinegar, parsley, dill seed, sugar and mayonnaise. Beat the mixture well and pour over salad. Add asparagus, chopped, and toss the salad. Serve to accompany cold meats, tinned fish or canned prawns.

Offshore salad

A salad of vegetables which will keep fresh for some days stored aboard. It has eye appeal, can be made in advance and is an excellent constituent of passage-making meals.

½ small cauliflower
1 cup shredded cabbage
1½ cups canned peas, drained
1 carton cress
¼ cup finely chopped onion
¼ pint of ½ and ½ mixture of mayonnaise and french dressing
1 carrot grated
1 cup cut beans canned (or dehydrated cooked) drained
1 cup chopped celery
Sprinkle of paprika

In advance
Cook cauliflower in boiling salt water (sea water diluted with fresh) until barely tender. Drain and allow to cool. When cold, marinade the cauliflower in french dressing (2 of oil to 1 of wine vinegar, beaten) turning the florets so that they are well coated. Leave for 2 hours. To prepare the salad, toss the cabbage with the peas, onion, grated carrot, cress, celery and beans, adding salt and pepper to taste. Blend French

dressing and mayonnaise, sprinkle over salad, mix and toss. Add the cauliflower florets to garnish and sprinkle with paprika.

Lemon slaw

3 cups shredded white cabbage
1 unpeeled red apple, cored and diced
¼ pint mixture of equal parts chopped green pepper and chopped spring onions
2 tablespoons dry white wine
½ teaspoon castor sugar

Dressing
3 hard boiled egg yolks
1 teaspoon dry mustard
½ tablespoon sugar
1 tablespoon salad oil
1 teaspoon grated lemon peel
½ tablespoon lemon juice
½ tablespoon single cream

Toss cabbage, apple, green pepper and onions with the sugar while adding the white wine. Mix and beat together egg yolks, mustard, sugar, oil, lemon juice and lemon peel. Fold in the cream. Whip this dressing and pour over the salad. Toss and serve. Makes a crisp, colourful piquant salad.

Starting gun salad

A quicky, both to prepare and to eat as a starter.

1½ cups cooked green peas (or canned peas) drained
1 cup sliced celery
3 hard boiled eggs, chopped
¼ pint mayonnaise
4 oz. chopped peanuts
3 tomatoes, sliced

Mix peas, celery and chopped egg. Make servings of this mix, top with spoonfuls of mayonnaise. Sprinkle with peanuts and garnish with tomato slices. A good accompaniment to a selection of cold smoked sausages.

Brazilian salad

¼ lb skinned tomatoes (or canned)
2 oz. pineapple pieces
Juice of ½ lemon
½ celery heart, chopped
½ lettuce heart, shredded
1 teaspoon single cream
Cayenne pepper to taste

Slice tomatoes, mix with celery heart and pineapple pieces. Shred lettuce heart (or cabbage) and mix with other ingredients. Pour over the mix in the bowl, the lemon juice and cream with a shake of cayenne pepper. Garnish with pineapple cubes.

Salad dressings

Low calorie dressing
This dressing, since it contains no oil, is popular with calorie watchers.

½ pint cider vinegar
1 tablespoon tomato ketchup
1 tablespoon chilli sauce
3 or 4 tablespoons water
2 tablespoons brown sugar
½ teaspoon minced garlic
½ teaspoon dry mustard
¼ teaspoon paprika
¼ teaspoon black pepper
1 saltspoon salt

Place all ingredients in a bowl and mix well. A quick way of mixing the ingredients, solid and liquid, for dressings and marinades, is to place them in a screw-topped bottle, fasten securely and shake vigorously. Afloat it is easier to do this than whip or stir in a bowl, which may be in motion already.

Vinaigrette dressing

2 hard boiled egg yolks
6 tablespoons salad oil
3 tablespoons vinegar (wine vinegar preferably)
2 spring onions, chopped finely
Salt and black pepper to taste

Mash yolks to a paste with the vinegar. Gradually blend in the oil, a little at a time, mixing well. Add the remaining ingredients and mix well. Serve as an additive to asparagus, broccoli or salad greens.

Thousand island dressing

½ pint mayonnaise
1 tablespoon chopped sweet pickle
1 hard boiled egg, finely chopped
¼ pint whipped single cream
2 tablespoons chilli sauce
2 tablespoons chopped pimento stuffed olives
½ teaspoon grated onion

Mix ingredients as they are, added in the order given. Makes about 1 pint of dressing.

Section 15

Eggs

For sheer economy of packaging with concentration of nutriment, there can be few sources of natural food to equal the egg. Of course walrus liver, seal blubber and turtle steaks are reputed to be rivals, but their source of supply is remote, especially when sailing en famille. The egg may also be regarded as an item for the medicine chest aboard, for a raw egg beaten with a good tot of brandy and a shake of cayenne pepper, taken at a swallow can revive and sustain a flagging crew, whose resistance to exposure will decrease in direct ratio to their confidence in the skipper and increase according to the cook's supply of egg nogs. One could in preparation for a long cruise emulate Cook, John Paul Jones and Nelson and carry one's own live egg factory en voyage, but accommodation-wise it is perhaps easier to store the eggs after laying.

The process for the preservation of fresh eggs is simple. Buy the eggs new laid and unwashed. This rules out supermarkets, but there are plenty of farms on country roads advertising fresh eggs which will meet the special requirements for storage. The fresher the eggs the better, obviously; unwashed they must be since the porous shells absorb water and rot sets in. If really fresh the shells should feel slightly rough. Prepare a sufficiency of egg boxes, the ½-dozen size is best. Coat each egg with a thin layer of petroleum jelly. A dessertspoonful of grease rubbed between the palms of the hands is enough for ½-dozen eggs. The appearance of the shell will change in the light as it is covered. Wrap each greased egg in tissue paper. Pack the tissue-wrapped greased eggs in the egg boxes, fasten each with Sellotape, and date each box to distinguish them. Store the eggs in the coolest area of the bilges next the skin. Eggs treated in this manner have been fresh 10 weeks after storage, despite a change from spring frost to tropical summer. With so many recipes which either start with or include four eggs, it is advisable to think of storage in terms of dozens.

It is also quite simple to preserve eggs, for immediate eating, by pickling. Two pickled eggs, a piece of cheese, half an onion with a hunk of buttered new crusty bread and a feast is in hand in the open air. A gargle or two of red wine and a song will undoubtedly emerge. Eggs for pickling should first be hard boiled, and since hard boiled eggs occur as components of so many menus, a word here on the cooking of eggs in the shell would seem appropriate.

Yours not to scoff, for that innocent looking object, the egg, is as touchy in the cooking as a booby-trapped copy of *Playboy* and as invitingly disappointing. Boiled for more than 3 minutes and the egg is not 'soft' nor is it hard either. To boil an egg so that the golden yolk lies liquidly in a firm white surround needs care and accuracy. First borrow the navigator's stop-watch. Then bring the water in the saucepan to the boil. When the water is bubbling furiously slide the eggs into the water via a cooking spoon so that they are totally immersed. When *the water boils and bubbles once more* give the eggs just 4 minutes (hence the navigator's timepiece). Remove the eggs immediately, tap the shell to crack, and serve – result perfection.

For hard boiled eggs the process should proceed for 10 minutes of boiling. At the end of this period remove the eggs and immediately plunge them into cold sea water. After 10 minutes change the water. When the eggs are quite cold a tap on the egg and the shell should peel away cleanly. If not chilled immediately, the membrane sticks the white of the egg to the shell and pieces of shell adhere to the shell fragments while peeling. Hard boiled eggs placed in heated preserving jars and topped with hot, pickling spiced vinegar will, if screw cap sealed, keep for a season, unless the jar is opened, when all the eggs disappear as by magic.

The omelette

It would appear that ever since there have been eggs there have been omelettes. For the omelette is the egg for all seasons, for any meal at any time on any day. Suited to all courses from entrée to dessert, prepared quickly or fussed over in complication, it has been cooked in its own peculiar national way by the French, Spanish, Italians, Germans, Russians, Greeks and Chinese. Even the British and their ex-colonial descendants have been known to make omelettes! There has yet to be the last word on this paragon of dishes.

For the lone sailor, for the family afloat, it is the ideal dish to serve for its versatility comes from both the method of cooking and from the multitude of ingredients which will so tastefully ring the changes upon its basic component, the whisked egg. The contents of almost any can of preserved food, the left-overs from many dishes, the local delicacies caught alive, will all serve to stretch, to enliven, to enhance the omelette. Here is the basic, step-by-step method of cooking a plain omelette. For four people, for four normal servings, take six–eight eggs.

1. *Beat the eggs with a fork for 30 seconds. If a light frothy omelette is required, 30 seconds of beating is enough. If a more homogenous, rubbery omelette is preferred, beat with a whisk for as long as it lasts! Thirty seconds with a fork is equal to 120 strokes and tiring on the wrist.
2. Stir in 1 tablespoon of cold water, add $\frac{1}{4}$ teaspoon salt and a pinch of pepper.
3. Heat the pan.
4. *When the pan is so hot that butter sizzles at the touch, melt a generous tablespoon butter in the pan.
5. *When the butter is foaming, put in a measure of the beaten egg mixture.
6. After 10 seconds stir lightly with a fork.
7. *As the omelette shapes, tilt the pan away lifting the edge of the omelette with the fork. Tilt the pan in the op-

posite direction and let the raw egg run into the pan. Keep shaking pan back and forth to keep the omelette free.

8. When cooked but still soft and frothy on top, turn the left side of the omelette to the centre with the fork. Slide the omelette to the right side of the pan well to the edge and turn out in three folds on to a warm plate.

The crucial stages are marked with an asterisk. The whisking process and the length of cooking time at stage 8 determine the consistency of the omelette. The over-whipped, over-cooked pseudo gasket material does not deserve the name omelette. Three basic continental recipes follow.

The mousseline omelette

Particularly suited to sweet fruit fillings, as a dessert dish.

1. Separate whites from yolks of 4 eggs.
2. Beat yolks well with 1 tablespoon of single cream until they thicken and turn pale.
3. Beat whites well until they stiffen enough to stand up in peaks, no more.
4. Fold yolks and whites together.
5. Melt 2½ tablespoons of butter in the pan and when sizzling, pour in the eggs.
6. Bring outer edge of omelette to the centre with a spoon until consistent, shaking the pan horizontally all the time to prevent omelette sticking.
7. Fold out double on to a warmed plate.

If a sweet omelette is required add 6 tablespoons of sugar and ½ teaspoon vanilla essence to the yolks. A creamy frothy light dessert should result.

A German omelette

This resembles somewhat the British pancake and is admirably suited to be spread with purées of tomatoes or mushrooms with liver sausage or a savoury mix and rolled to accompany a meat dish.

1. Into 2 tablespoons of fine flour in a bowl, stir, one at a time, 3 whole eggs.
2. Add ½ cup single cream, salt and pepper to taste and a pinch of grated nutmeg. Whisk until smooth.
3. Melt 1 teaspoon of butter in the pan and when sizzling pour in ½ egg batter. Reduce heat.
4. Keep heat moderate and shake pan to prevent sticking.
5. When slightly brown on one side, slide omelette on to warm plate and keep warm.
6. Re-butter pan and repeat process with other half of mixture.
7. Spread omelettes with honey or cranberry jelly, roll each and serve to accompany gammon rashers or pork fillet.

The Italian frittata

The frittata is a basic omelette, but the filling of diced ham, tomato, cooked green pepper, peas or salami is mixed with the whisked egg before pouring into the pan. The frittata is browned on both sides. To achieve the culinary dexterity required in turning the omelette, place an enamel plate upside down over the omelette, when almost cooked, in the pan. Hold pan and plate together and smartly turn pan upside down. The omelette now on the plate may be slipped back into the pan to brown its other side. It is advisable to use an enamel plate, as they are relatively unbreakable. Omelette may be removed from hair, books, bulkheads and sleeping bags with warm water. Since filling ingredients are incorporated with the whisked egg, the mixture is likely to stick, so horizontal shaking is an essential to the process.

Recipes for omelette fillings

Kippered herrings

1 cup kipper fillets, canned (or any smoked fish).

Flake the fish. Heat in 1 tablespoon of butter and add 2 tablespoons of double cream. Stir until thoroughly mixed and heated. Fold this mixture into a basic 6-egg omelette, sprinkle with paprika and serve.

Omelette albina

½ onion, finely chopped
3 small mushrooms sliced
1 tablespoon butter
½ cup chicken stock (stock cube)
1 teaspoon fine flour
½ cup minced chicken (canned chicken breast)
6 eggs
1 tablespoon butter
3 tablespoons cream
1 teaspoon sherry
1 teaspoon oregano

Sauté the onions and mushrooms in butter. Add the minced chicken and blend in the flour. Heat half of the chicken stock and add this to the onion, mushroom, chicken, flour mix and simmer for 3 minutes, adding 1 teaspoon of sherry at the last. To other half of chicken stock add cream and oregano and heat. Cook the basic 6-egg omelette and fill this with the chicken hash. Fold omelette and serve on hot plate. Pour over cream sauce.

Omelette béarnaise

1 onion, chopped
1 sweet pimento, chopped
½ cup diced ham
1 large peeled tomato, chopped
1 tablespoon parsley
1 tablespoon bacon fat (from breakfast)
6 eggs

Prepare the basic 6-egg omelette. Sauté in the bacon fat the onion, pimento and tomato. Simmer this for 5 minutes. Fold this mixture into the omelette, serve, garnished liberally with parsley.

The tinned meats and shell fish, shrimps, prawns, crab and such vegetable delights as asparagus and artichoke hearts all make delicious fillings for omelettes which may then serve as the main course of the meal. The accentuation of taste by the addition of a little of 'this and that' makes all the difference.

Section 16

Fish

The pattern of fish food ashore could often be described as 'rectangular, boiled, fried or fish cake'. What a world of difference is at the ship's cook's command. As a food fish is rich in protein, phosphorous and vitamins. For those who are quick to the bottle and slow to table at meal times there are innumerable fish dishes which, prepared beforehand, can be kept to be lifted to table at the last minute. Yet fish is still not the most popular of foodstuffs. The dislike probably stems from the traditional 'fish on Fridays' syndrome, so that fish is regarded as a penance. There is also the anti-fish reaction caused by smell, bones, slimy skin and the texture of cotton wool. These prejudices can be dealt with summarily. Smell can be avoided if the fish is wrapped in foil or a plastic bag to poach. It should never be boiled hard, for it is the belting with bubbling boiling water which produces the smell and the cotton-wool texture. If hands and pans smell of fish, a mere rubbing with a piece of lemon will remove all odour. As for bones and slimy skin, set aside and forego herrings, trout, mackerel and mullet and only a central bone remains in most of the edible fishy world. Buy plaice, sole and kippers filleted and bones will no longer bother – taste will be lost with them, too! As for the wet cotton wool allegation, the responsibility for this can be placed on the pre-packaged preparation of frozen fish steaks with a so called sauce; this is so frequently improperly defrosted, heated too fast in cooking and dished up without care that cotton wool and wallpaper paste must result. No sailing man need suffer such indignity at table for he shares the fishes' natural environment and the fisherman's harbour. So troll for mackerel, line for bass or dive for lobsters and if out of luck follow the local catch to market as the boats come in. The selection on most coasts is a constant source of delight.

When choosing fish from the slab, first look the beast in the eye. It should return the gaze bright and clear. If the eyes are sunken grey holes in a corpse, reject the body. The gills should be bright red and moist, not nicotine yellow brown slits and the skin should be unbroken. The flesh of cutlets should be translucent, firm and elastic, with a close grain. If asking the seller to fillet the fish, demand the head, tail and fins. They have been paid for and are excellent material for a sauce if poached or braised fish is planned. Fresh fish should have no smell. The slimy skin dislike may be allayed by having the purchase skinned in the market. Or, do it aboard.

To skin the fish, first wash it in clean sea water. If too near the local sewer outfall, wash it in salted fresh water. For a round fish, cut round each pectoral fin (the forward end pair) right and left, just behind the gills. Slit the skin across below the head. Loosen the skin along the abdomen and pull backwards towards the tail. Repeat on the other side.

For a flat fish, skin from the tail towards the head. Start with the dark side uppermost making an incision across just above the tail. Lift the skin and pull towards the head, using the thumb to loosen the skin. Repeat the process with the other side. If in difficulty use the pliers from the tool kit to get a firm grip. Skin may be removed from fillets by laying the fish, skin down, on a board and slipping a sharp knife between fish and skin. Cleaning fish need not be a messy business, if the knife is large and sharp and if the operation is performed on newsprint or greaseproof paper laid on a board. With round fish make an incision across the fish below the head. Make a second cut from this incision along the abdomen to the vent, bend the head back and scrape out the guts on to the paper. Put the cleaned fish in a bowl of salted water, wipe the knife on the paper, screw up the guts in the used sheet and discard. There should be no blood on the deck or the cook at the conclusion of the operation. To clean flat fish make a curved incision from behind the gills to the vent and scrape out guts as before.

To fillet flat fish, lay the fish on the paper-covered board with the tail towards you. Make an incision from head to tail towards you, along the line of the backbone. Then working from tail to head shave off the left-hand fillet from left to right. Turn the fish round and repeat for the right-hand fillet. Turn the fish over and repeat the process for the other side. Wash the fillets in salted water. To fillet round fish, slit the back down the centre line from head to tail. Follow this first cut, paring diagonally across the fish to remove the fillet from each side.

If the fish is large and is to be served whole, cut off the pectoral and basal fins with the kitchen scissors, but leave the dorsal fin (the large fin along the back) until the fish is cooked; it will then come away from the spine easily. To scale a fish, e.g. red mullet, work from the tail to the head, against the grain, scraping with the knife edge. Do not scrape too vigorously as this spreads the scales all over the area and they are difficult to remove from surfaces other than fish skin. Finally, if fish has to be kept for up to 24 hours without refrigeration, wrap it in a cloth soaked in half and half mixture of vinegar and water and place in a plastic container in the bilges.

Cooking fish

Fish, like eggs, need to be cooked quickly at a high temperature. Once the flesh is opaque throughout, it is cooked. If it is to be fried, the temperature of the oil should be about 135° C. In a deep fry this means that a small cube of bread thrown into the heated oil should rise to the surface and turn brown in a few seconds. To be braised, fish should be cooked, with the prepared vegetables in a prepared stock called a court bouillon or a fumet. Poaching is a simple and very digestable way of cooking fish. It should be simmered gently in a court bouillon or milk until the flesh is opaque throughout. If poached in milk the process will take just as long as the milk does to boil. Do not allow the dish to boil, uncovered, for a long time, the flesh will lose its juices and cotton wool will result. The kitchen too, will smell as the bubbles burst on the air.

The quickest and tastiest way of cooking fish is wrapped in foil and pot roasted in the pressure cooker. The washed and trimmed fish is placed on a buttered sheet of metal foil, with a few rings of onion, a little chopped carrot and a pinch of dill and powdered mace. A knob of butter and a tablespoon of Pernod or white vermouth is added. The foil is folded round the fish and the edges are rolled to seal. The package is then pot roasted in the cooker. The foil retains the tastes and aromas, and fish served in this manner is food for the gods. The result of any poaching or boiling process for fish is enhanced if the liquid used is a court bouillon or fumet. The term court bouillon is used for either of the following mixtures.

1. Simmer together 3 glasses of water, 2 glasses of milk, 1 tablespoon salt, 4 peppercorns, a bay leaf and a slice of lemon. Strain and use the liquid.
2. Simmer together 4 glasses of water, 1 glass of dry white wine, 1 tablespoon of salt, 4 peppercorns, a pinch of thyme, a tablespoon of parsley, 3 mushrooms, sliced, 1 small onion, sliced, 1 carrot, sliced, 1 head of celery, chopped. Strain and use the liquid.

If you prefer the fish may be cooked in a fumet. This is prepared by adding to the strained liquid in (1) or (2) above, the heads, tails, fins, bones and trimmings of the fish. Simmer this for not more than 20 minutes. Longer cooking will turn the liquid bitter. Strain the cooked mixture and use as a cooking liquid for the fish. If to every pint of the strained liquid 2 tablespoons of cooked rice are added together with the yolks of 2 eggs and a tablespoon of lemon juice, the whole will make an excellent fish soup.

Grilled fish

Fish such as herrings, mackerel, sardines and pilchards should be grilled. Under the grill the skins crisp and the flesh cooks within, remaining white. White fish such as sole, plaice, mullet, bass, trout and salmon also are delicious if grilled. The flesh must be well basted with butter during the cooking process. The flavour is much improved if the fish is treated first in one of the following ways:

1. Brushed with melted butter and dipped in savoury flour.
2. Sprinkled with oil and coated with mustard.

3. Brushed with oil and dipped in coarse oatmeal.
4. Wrapped in rashers of bacon.

Fish which has been marinaded is delicious if grilled (for marinades see section 8).

Pan fried fish

Fish with a delicate taste such as trout, sole or plaice are tasty if just pan fried in butter. Fillets of large fish, cod, haddock, hake or tuna may be coated with beaten egg yolk and breadcrumbs before frying. The larger steaks of fish are much improved if coated and left to stand for half an hour in the following mixture. To 1 tablespoon anchovy sauce, 1 crushed clove of garlic, 2 teaspoons of mixed herbs, a pinch of cayenne pepper and a teaspoon of mustard add 2 tablespoons of olive oil, a little at a time, stirring continuously. Coat the fish liberally with this mix and leave to stand. After 30 minutes fry gently, shaking the pan to prevent sticking. The herb mix recommended for the process consists of equal portions of tarragon, chervil, dill, fennel and thyme.

Deep frying

Deep frying afloat should be embarked upon with caution for it can be dangerous. The potential for scalding and the danger of fire is a constant hazard. Even moored in a marina one is not safe from the slap-happy, semi-inebriate who leaps without warning across the foredeck to reach his, the outside boat. However, with caution, in a proper deep-fry pan with basket and lid, fish and chips may be attempted. The pan must never be more than one third full of oil, the cook must wear an apron and oven gloves and a piece of heavy duty canvas should be to hand to douse the flames in emergency. The following points must be observed:

1. NEVER DEEP FRY UNDER WAY.
2. NEVER DEEP FRY IN UNSTABLE CONDITIONS.
3. NEVER USE WATER ON A FAT FIRE.

Preparation for deep fried fish

Cut the fish into even-sized pieces so that it will cook uniformly. Coat the fish in one of the following mixes:

1. Dip the fish in salted milk. Prepare a seasoned flour in a greaseproof bag. Shake the milked fish in the bag to coat with flour.
2. Beat an egg with 1 teaspoon each of oil and water. Dip the fish in salted milk then in the egg mix. Allow the fish to drag across the lip of the dish to remove surplus egg. Roll in dried frying crumbs.
3. Mix in a bowl 1 cup of fine flour, 1 tablespoon of oil, 2 egg yolks, a shake of salt and pepper and ¼ pint of milk or beer (mild ale is best). Fold into this mixture the whites of the eggs beaten to a snow. Wipe the fish dry with a paper towel and dip in the batter.

The fat for deep frying fish should be between 170°–190° C though whitebait requires a temperature of 200° C. Fat for deep frying must not smoke. If it is too hot it will burn and turn brown and is then spoiled for cooking. An immediate reaction with the bread-cube test is a good indication of a satisfactory temperature. When the fat is hot enough place the coated pieces of fish in the basket and lower into the fat. Place the lid on the pan immediately. A golden colour in the coating is a fair indication that the fish is done.

Chips should first be fried at a lower temperature to cook for 7 minutes until soft. Lift the chips in the basket and raise the fat temperature to 190° C. Return the chips to the hot fat and finish cooking. Drain both fish and chips on paper towels.

To sauté fish with cream

Take fillets or steaks of any white fish. First flatten the fish with a spatula or large cooking knife, and sprinkle with lemon juice and a pinch of salt. Place 1 tablespoon of butter in the pan and allow to melt. Cook fish in the pan for 5 minutes but do not allow it to brown. Add 1 teacupful of chopped parsley, 3 tablespoons of cream and a sprinkle of fresh milled pepper; or add 3 tablespoons fresh cream, 1 tablespoon of French mustard and 2 teaspoons of lemon juice. Finish cooking without boiling. Serve.

Herring (or mackerel) with mustard sauce

4 large herring or mackerel
4 soft roes
2 tablespoons of oil

Keep the roes aside, clean the fish, rub with salt and pepper, brush with oil. Cook in the frying pan or under the grill for 7 minutes. Remove and keep warm in a dish.

Mustard Sauce

2 tablespoons butter
4 tablespoons cream
2 egg yolks
2 tablespoons fresh mustard
1 tablespoon lemon juice
Salt and pepper to taste

Put the roes through a sieve and whip the other ingredients of the sauce with the roes. Heat in a small saucepan in a larger saucepan of boiling water (called a bain marie!). Reduce heat, and stir continuously for the sauce must not boil. Pour sauce over cooked fish in its dish. Serve with well-buttered potatoes, cooked in their jackets.

Fillets of fish with bacon, tomatoes and mushrooms

1 tablespoon of oil
4 rashers of bacon
4 fillets of flat fish (about 2 lb)

Oil the pan and fry the rashers on both sides. Lift out the bacon and keep. Sauté the fish in the bacon fat.

Take:
2 tomatoes
8 mushrooms
2 teaspoons oil
1 tablespoon lemon juice
½ glass white wine
Salt and pepper to taste

Cut each rasher into 2 and arrange bacon and fish in an oven-proof dish with a lid. Surround fish with tomatoes, sliced and chopped mushrooms. Sprinkle this with lemon juice and oil and add white wine. Cover with lid and cook slowly over an asbestos mat, or grill without lid for 20 minutes. Serve with asparagus and cream sauce.

Bream with fennel

Clean and scale the fish. Fill the inside of the fish with French mustard to which a few fennel seeds have been added. Score the skin of the fish with three or four ⅛-in. deep cuts on each side. Sprinkle these cuts with fennel seeds. Dot the fish with butter and wrap in foil, folding the edges to seal. Place on the trivet of the pressure cooker and cook under pressure for 20 minutes.

Tuna macaroni casserole

4 oz. can tuna or salmon, drained and broken into pieces

1 cup cooked macaroni, drained
½ cup milk
¼ teaspoon celery seed
½ tablespoon butter
½ can cream of celery soup
½ lb Cheddar cheese, grated
1 tablespoon chopped onion

Sauté the onion in the hot butter. When clear add the soup and the milk, stirring slowly. Fold in the tuna, the celery seed and half of the grated cheese. Mix in the macaroni. Place the whole in a buttered casserole, with lid. Top with the remaining cheese.

Heat casserole, with lid on, over an asbestos mat for 15 minutes or until cheese melts. Serve with green peppers, cubed and fried in butter.

Grilled scallops provençal

Wash and trim the scallops cutting out everything but the white and orange parts. Drain and dry on a paper towel. Simmer scallops in half and half dry wine and water for 10 minutes. Remove and cut in quarters. In a pan heat 1 tablespoon of butter, toss in the pan chopped shallots, chopped mushrooms and a tablespoon of parsley. Add the scallops, stir in a little flour to absorb fat and then add the cooking liquid from the scallops. Stir and heat until the liquid thickens. Serve with artichoke hearts, piled into the cup halves of the shells.

Jambala

8 scampi or large prawns
2 tablespoons butter
1 tablespoon oil
3 onions, chopped
1 cup cubed ham
2 cloves garlic
3 tomatoes, skinned and chopped
1 green pepper, chopped
2 cups cooked rice
½ bay leaf
½ teaspoon thyme
Pinch of cayenne pepper
Dash of Worcester sauce
1 cup mussel meats
2 cups chicken stock

Chop the scampi/prawns. Heat the butter and oil in an oven-proof casserole over an asbestos mat. Cook the onions until clear. Add the ham, the scampi or prawns and after a few minutes the chopped garlic, tomatoes, mushrooms, peppers, herbs and rice. Stir with the seasoning. Pour over the chicken stock and close the lid. Cook for 12 minutes. Add the mussel meats and cook for a further 3 minutes. To serve, pour over each portion 1 tablespoon sherry.

Grand Central Station clam stew

Use canned clams and clam juice, mussels, small oysters or cockles
1 tablespoon butter
½ teaspoon celery salt
½ teaspoon paprika
½ teaspoon Worcester sauce
¾ cup clam juice
½ cup shelled fish, drained
1½ cups milk

Heat butter and the seasoning in a pan, pour in the clam juice and simmer for a few minutes. Add the shell fish and as soon as the edges turn, add the milk. Bring to the boil and lift from the heat. Put a knob of butter in each soup bowl, pour over the soup and add a sprinkle of paprika.

No host skipper should ever leave any of the guests at risk on their return journey . . .

Section 17

Meat

Meat preservation by marinading

This culinary process, which sounds like a seagoing evolution, gets its name from a brine made to conserve meat. It has an obvious nautical association with the casks of salt beef and pork which constituted the staple diet of the 18th-century sailor. Part of the purpose of the marinade is to preserve the meat over a period by stopping the process of decomposition which meat and fish will undergo with time, and at the same time to tenderise and flavour the flesh. Much used historically to treat freshly killed meat of hunted animals, wild boar, deer and hare, marinades are now employed to give this 'wild' taste to lamb, rabbit, pork and beef and to add spice to those fish which have little naturally.

Marinades all have a basis of wine or vinegar to which herbs, spices and vegetables are added. The marinades can be used raw, as prepared, or cooked in which case they must be allowed to cool before use. In marinading there is always an exchange of flavours between the marinade and the treated meat or fish, which explains why it is usual to take a little of the marinade to make the sauce which will accompany the cooked dish. The change of taste which occurs in the process is almost miraculous. Fillet of pork becomes wild boar, lamb is changed to venison, while rabbit is translated into jugged hare.

Raw marinades are used to season rather than tenderise meat so these processes are relatively short. Cooked marinades on the other hand, are used for tenderising and the process takes much longer. Every 3 or 4 days cooked marinade must be reheated, the meat being removed during this part of the operation. For the ship's cook's use, marinades will most often be raw, lasting some 24 hours or so. For larger pieces of beef or pork, the cooked marinade may take up to a week.

The rules for success are few but essential.

1. Metal dishes or pans must never be used. Earthenware or oven-proof glass are essential.
2. The joints must be completely covered by the liquid.
3. During the process the meat or fish must be turned and basted using a wooden spoon.
4. A cooked marinade must be quite cold before use.
5. A cooked marinade must be reheated every 4 days.
6. In any raw marinade, place half of the vegetables in the bottom of the dish, put the meat or fish on top and cover with the rest of the vegetables. Pour the liquid over the whole. Cover with a lid.

Raw white wine marinade for beef (2 lb meat)

3 onions in slices
1 carrot cut in rounds
1 teaspoon thyme
2 bay leaves
2 cloves crushed garlic
1 teaspoon salt
¼ pint olive oil
½ bottle dry white wine
1 teaspoon lemon juice

Leave meat in marinade, covered, for 12 hours. Turn, baste and leave for further 24 hours.

Pacific marinade for pork

1 cup soy sauce
1 clove chopped garlic
1 tablespoon minced onion
2 tablespoons lemon juice
1 tablespoon sherry
1 teaspoon ground ginger
1 tablespoon brown treacle
¼ cup demerara sugar
1 cup white wine

Proceed as in rules 2, 3 and 6.

An Indo-Chinese marinade for chicken

½ cup olive oil
½ cup dry white wine
½ cup demerara sugar
1 teaspoon ground ginger
1 cup soy sauce
⅓ cup spring onion tops, chopped (or chives)
6 coriander seeds

Proceed as in rules 2, 3 and 6

Poacher's marinade for rabbit

2 cups red wine
1 cup olive oil
1 cup wine vinegar
2 onions, sliced
3 cloves garlic, chopped
2 bay leaves
6 peppercorns
1 tablespoon parsley, chopped
1 sliced lemon
½ cup currants

Proceed as in rules 2, 3 and 6.

The great advantage of the process to those feeding aboard is the preservation, even if only for a few days, of the life of unrefrigerated meat. In a well-sealed container, the marinaded meat in the liquid may be carried aboard already prepared, and with attention to turning can be cooked 3 or

4 days later. Meats from the marinade may be grilled, fried, braised or roasted in the normal manner. The treatment, in principle, may be extended to fresh fruit. Wash and dry the fruit and steep in the marinade for some 4 hours, in a sealed plastic container: raspberries in a mix of $\frac{1}{4}$ cup of port and $\frac{1}{4}$ cup of brandy; sliced strawberries in $\frac{1}{4}$ cup fresh orange juice, $\frac{1}{4}$ cup brandy, $\frac{1}{4}$ cup honey; melon cubes with a dusting of ginger and a cup of Sauterne wine.

Pot roasting for meat dishes

Meat recipes for the boats' galley consist of methods of using simple cuts of fresh meat with the simplest ways of cooking, such as frying, grilling or braising. Canned meat can only be treated in the same way for there are, after all, only three ways of cooking anything, with hot air, with hot oil or with hot water. Whether fried, boiled or baked the tastiest dishes made aboard from either fresh or canned ingredients have one important ingredient in common – imagination, which, with enthusiasm, characterises the skilled cook. Even if deprived of an oven, those addicted to a carved joint of meat may be served their beef pot roasted.

The method consists of first sealing the meat in hot fat to keep in the juices and give an attractive appearance. The meat is then cooked instead very quickly, softening and tenderising the flesh. Joints of up to $2\frac{1}{2}$ lb can be pot roasted and the best choice is the cheapest cuts. Of beef, choose shin or topside; in mutton, the leg or middle neck; and in veal or pork, the best end of neck or fillet. Melt sufficient oil in the open pressure cooker to cover the bottom. Heat until just smoking, put in the joint and brown it well, turning frequently on all sides. Lift out the meat, take the pot from the heat and pour off the fat. Add $\frac{3}{4}$ pint of stock (beef or chicken for veal, pork or lamb). Put the trivet into the pot, dust the meat with salt and pepper and return it for cooking under pressure for 15 minutes. Reduce the pressure, open the cooker and place the raw vegetables for the menu, prepared in the cooker separators. Bring the cooker to pressure once more and cook for a further 5 minutes. The great advantages here are that the toughest meat will be cooked tender, the cuts can therefore be cheaper, secondly the whole course of meat and vegetables may be cooked on one burner alone and thirdly that the whole process including preparation should not occupy more than three quarters of an hour.

Recipes with canned meats

Few small cruisers have ice-boxes or refrigerators large enough to hold fresh meat for a crew of four for more than a day or two. In temperate climates meat will keep fresh for 2 or 3 days, if brought aboard frozen. In warm climates in summer it would not be safe to keep meat for more than a few hours. Some solution can be found in the marinade but it is to canned materials which are readily available and easily stored, that the cook must turn most often. As an example, try:

Ham madeira

1 oz. butter
1 teaspoon paprika
$\frac{1}{2}$ sliced cooked ham (canned)
$\frac{1}{2}$ pint water
2 tablespoons tomato soup powder
A pinch of nutmeg
1 glass Madeira or sweet sherry

Melt the butter and mix to a paste with the soup powder, paprika and nutmeg. Add water gradually stirring to reconstitute the mixture, return to the heat and boil. (Tomato purée or concentrated tomato soup serve equally well.)

Lightly grill the ham slices, basting with a little butter. Place in a dish. To the boiling tomato sauce, add the wine, stir and pour over the ham slices. Serve garnished with slices of tomato.

A very easy, very quick and delicious-tasting simple dish from readily available meat and ingredients.

Beefburgers with wine sauce

1 large tin beefburgers
½ oz. cooking fat or oil
4 mushrooms
1 teaspoon chopped parsley
4 long streaky rashers of bacon
4 small onions
4 tablespoons red wine
½ tablespoon fine flour

Separate the beefburgers. De-rind the bacon and stretch each rasher with the back of a kitchen knife on a board. Roll the beefburgers and wrap the bacon round them, pinning with a cocktail stick. Heat the oil or fat in a pan and fry the beefburgers. Remove from the pan, drain on paper towels and keep warm in a dish. Chop the onions and slice the mushrooms, add fat to the pan and sauté gently for 4 minutes. Stir in the flour and then add the wine to the pan. Bring to the boil, adding the parsley. Pour the sauce over the beefburger rolls and serve with creamed potatoes and haricot beans.

Rognons Carolina

4 kidneys (or a large tin of kidneys)
1 tablespoon parsley, salt and pepper to taste
1 clove garlic, crushed, not chopped
1 liqueur glass Cognac
2 shallots, chopped
1 teaspoon Dijon mustard
½ glass white wine
1 tablespoon butter

Chop the kidneys, shallots, add the parsley. In an oven-proof glassware dish, melt the butter. Add the crushed clove of garlic, and stir. After a few seconds, add the chopped kidney and seasoning. Cook on an asbestos mat over a burner turning the kidneys from time to time. Heat the brandy in a soup ladle, flame and pour over the kidneys. Add the wine and cook rapidly for 3 minutes. Remove the garlic clove, sprinkle with chives and serve hot, with rice and artichoke hearts.

Chicken casserole

For the recipe frozen chicken joints, canned chicken breasts or whole tinned chicken may be used. If using canned vegetables, drain them first. 4 frozen joints of chicken or 1 large can chicken breasts or breast from tinned whole chicken.

Fry joints after thawing, or fry strips of chicken breast in a pan with butter, until golden. Transfer chicken to pressure cooker, with trivet in place.

1 onion, chopped
1 stick of celery, chopped
1 large tin garden peas
3 tomatoes, peeled and chopped
2 rashers streaky bacon, chopped
1 oz. butter
1 oz. fine flour
¼ pint chicken stock (chicken stock cube)
2 glasses white wine

Add butter to pan and fry bacon gently for 5 minutes. Sprinkle flour and pepper and salt to taste to the pan, add tomatoes and stock and stir until boiling. Pour the boiling mixture over the chicken in the pressure cooker, add onion, celery and white wine, close cooker and bring to pressure. If chicken is fresh, cook for 20 minutes; if canned, cook for 10 minutes. Serve.

Beef Mexicano

2 tins stewed steak or $1\frac{1}{2}$ lb shin of beef
8 small onions
1 tablespoon oil
1 tablespoon ready mixed mustard
2 cloves garlic, chopped
1 tablespoon honey
1 large can peeled tomatoes
1 tablespoon sweet chutney
1 tablespoon blackcurrant jam

If using fresh meat, cut it in cubes, toss in seasoned flour, heat the oil in the pan and brown the meat all over, and use pressure cooker to complete the recipe, cooking for 25 minutes, with all ingredients added to the steak. If using chunky canned steak, blend well together tomatoes, mustard, garlic and all other ingredients and add to the steak in a pan. Cook well, stirring occasionally, for 10 minutes.

Section 18

Vegetables

The historical record of the great voyages of the early seafarers in their search for the ends of the earth is punctuated by the harrowing details of crews decimated by disease, starvation and thirst whilst away from land for months at a time. Tens of thousands of mariners perished before the elixir of life afloat was found in the minute trace substances, of which type C is found in fresh fruit and raw vegetables. A daily sip of fresh lemon juice, a nibble of potato peel, a crop of green cress, a breath of onion and teeth and joints are immune to the dread scourge of the long sea voyage, the scurvy.

Boiling and prolonged cooking destroys most of the essence, the vitamins, present in any food. Pressure cooking, probably because it is quicker, does not break down the vitamins to the same extent. Fresh fruit and fresh vegetables are vitamin full so the 'apples and greens' sections of the boat's larder are all important. Fresh air and fresh food are the greatest factors to well-being, anywhere, so when afloat shopping for fresh fruit and vegetables once a week is just common sense. Green vegetables, such as cabbage heart or cauliflower, and all the root vegetables, carrots, parsnips, turnips, swedes will keep for several days (a) in the cool (b) in well-ventilated conditions (c) if turned regularly and any defective items discarded. It is, of course, essential to buy sound stock to begin with. The conditions required for storage are often best met by suspending the fruit and vegetables in nylon nets under the ventilator of the loo! Light and easily stored dehydrated alternatives to fresh greenstuff are readily available. Tinned and canned varieties are found everywhere. The range of both types of preserved ready-to-serve material is considerable and may be justified in use by the limitations of availability. Their inclusion will never earn the ship's cook a medal or blue riband.

Recipes

The recipes which follow all concern fresh vegetables, easily kept for up to a week when cruising and all cooked in an interesting manner. They begin with the much maligned cabbage. The Victorian mother's adage 'not hungry for cabbage, not hungry for cake', was a dictum which founded the next and succeeding generations' dislike for 'greens'. But if you ever see a bull, with his cows, in a kale field, you will regard 'greens' in inverted commas or in any other manner, with a new respect.

This recipe may help to dispel a common dislike.

Stuffed cabbage rolls

8 large cabbage leaves
1 slice white bread
½ teaspoon mixed herbs
¼ pint beef stock (beef cube)
12 oz. can corned beef
1 egg, beaten
1 oz. butter

From a good-sized cabbage heart detach 8 large unbroken leaves. (Cut out the end of the leaf stem of each in turn and carefully roll off unbroken.) Wash these leaves thoroughly and place in boiling water for 3 minutes to soften. Remove and keep warm. Flake the corned beef with a knife. Crumble the bread into a basin and mix in the meat mixture to fill each cabbage leaf rolling up the leaf around the filling as a parcel. Melt the butter in a large frying pan and add the cabbage rolls, folds down, to the pan. Fry for 3 minutes, add the stock and simmer for 10 minutes. Serve hot.

Asparagus polonnaise

What better vegetable to succeed cabbage than asparagus. Fresh, it is delicious, canned, it can be transformed. Bought fresh in a coastal market, it is not too expensive and one may then eat it as does the President of the French Republic (and other high society) with one's fingers. Both white and green varieties may be found. The white kind should be peeled, the green does not need to be. Cut into even lengths and tied in small bunches, they should be put into shallow salted water to boil for some 12 minutes (in the pressure cooker for 6 minutes). The asparagus is cooked when soft but not limp. It can then be served à la polonnaise.

2 hard boiled eggs
2 teaspoons chopped parsley
4 oz. butter
1 oz. dried breadcrumbs
Salt and pepper to taste

Divide the yolks and whites of the eggs. Chop the yolks and mix with parsley. Melt the butter in a pan and fry the breadcrumbs until brown. Arrange the asparagus in an oven-proof dish, cover first with the egg/parsley mixture, then with the browned breadcrumbs and garnish with chopped white of egg.

French beans à la bourguignonne

2 lb French beans (1 can sliced green beans). If canned, heat and drain; if fresh, trim, cut and boil, uncovered, in salt water for 15 minutes or until tender.

5 oz. butter
4 teaspoons flour
½ pint stock (chicken stock cube)

¼ pint red wine
2 tablespoons fines herbes
Juice of ½ lemon

Heat half the butter in the pan, stir in the flour to make a roux. Stirring constantly gradually add the stock and wine and cook slowly until the mixture thickens. Pour into a heated jug and keep warm.

Heat the other half of the butter in the pan and sauté the cooked beans, with the fines herbes for 5 minutes. Add the wine sauce, stirring. Serve and sprinkle with lemon juice before serving.

Haricot beans with mushrooms

8 oz. mushrooms, chopped
3 medium-sized onions, chopped
2 lb beans (1 large can of beans)
1½ oz. butter
¼ pint double cream
2 teaspoons paprika

Cook the beans in salted water for 20 minutes or until just soft (drain the tinned beans). Heat the cooked beans in a pan with butter, and in another pan sauté the chopped onion and mushrooms in butter until onion is clear. Add beans with paprika and cream to the onion mushroom mix. Cook for further 5 minutes and serve.

Carrots à l'Andalouse

1 lb carrots (1 large tin cut carrots)

Cook the carrots in salted water and drain or heat the canned carrots and drain.

1½ oz. butter
1 teaspoon flour
1 teaspoon Cognac
1 teaspoon grated nutmeg
1 egg white, beaten stiff

Mash the carrots finely. Add ½ oz. butter, the flour, the Cognac and grated nutmeg. Mix and fold in the egg white. Heat the rest of the butter in a pan and lightly brown the carrot mixture. Serve from a heated dish.

Leeks à la grecque

2 lb young leeks
¼ pint chicken stock (chicken stock cube)
6 tablespoons white wine
3 tablespoons oil
1 tablespoon tomato purée
8 small onions
4 bay leaves
1 teaspoon peppercorns
1 teaspoon paprika

Remove all green from the leeks and cut into 1 in. pieces. Boil in salt water for 5 minutes. Drain.

Put the leeks into an open pan with all the ingredients except the paprika and simmer for 30 minutes. The liquid should be very concentrated at the end of this period. Sprinkle with paprika and serve. The dish can be left to cool and later served cold as an hors d'oeuvre.

Potatoes

The alternatives to fresh potatoes are so numerous and so simple as well as being easy to store, that the use of fresh potatoes with the need for bulk storage and the chore of peeling, is not recommended. For ways and means of serving dehydrated potatoes or frozen chips read the directions on the packets. However, as a suggestion, any dish of mashed potatoes is immeasurably improved by the addition of an avocado pear, peeled and diced. The cubes, mashed with a knob of butter into the potatoes, give an attractive new taste to an all too familiar dish.

Mark the stores clearly . . .

Section 19

Rice, pasta and curry

The cooking of rice seems to have acquired a mystique all of its own. Ranging from the studied casual remark, 'oh! just toss a handful into boiling water', to the expertise implied by the almost whispered, 'study the grains first', the ways, means and methods of cooking rice seem almost as legion as the grains themselves. However, all rice not thrown at newly married couples needs to be boiled in water until just tender. The water may be salted or the rice may be fried first, but ultimately must come the act of boiling to reach the narrow divide of perfection between the hard as bullets condition and a glutinous mush. Only trial and error with practice and vigilance can catch the rice after the grains have softened but before they split. Rice differs in type and appearance from the large pearly white grains of Carolina rice, usually served as a pudding to the long, thin grains and slightly brownish tinge of hard Patna rice superb with curries. The intermediate varieties from polished rice of Italy to the national types of Burma and Japan need not bother the cook in the galley unless the skipper served a long term in the Indian sub-continent or sailed a junk in the China seas.

There are two common methods of cooking rice. First as a measure, a cupful of rice is ample for two persons.

Method 1

First wash the grains in cold water until the water runs clear. Sea water may be used if far enough off shore and away from the tanker's track. This washing removes the fine flour present in all rice. Drain and place in the saucepan adding twice the volume of water (1 cupful of rice to 2 cupfuls of water). Bring to the boil over high heat. When boiling, turn off the heat and allow the rice to stand, in the saucepan with the lid on, for 3 minutes. Then with medium heat, simmer for about 15 minutes or until all the liquid has been absorbed or evaporated. Accurate timing of this is not possible as the quality of rice and the approximation of heat and quantities will alter circumstances. It is necessary to watch the final stages carefully. The rice should be tender, not soggy, the grains should be separate and the pot must not boil dry or the rice will stick and burn. Vigilance alone brings success. Remove the pan from the heat and wash the rice in cold water in a sieve. Put a knob of butter in the pan, return the rice to warm on an asbestos mat over low heat. The grains when served should be separate and tender.

Method 2. For hard rice

In Asian or curry dishes use a stock (beef or chicken cube) instead of water to cook the rice. Wash the rice and drain. Melt a little butter or oil in a pan over low heat. Add the rice, advance the heat and sauté the grains until the rice begins to brown. Stir while sauté proceeds but not too vigorously or the grains will be split or crushed. When the rice is brown add the stock, twice as much by volume as rice, and cook over high heat until boiling. Reduce heat and simmer, covering pan and continuing until all liquid is absorbed or evaporated. Serve from the pan.

A risotto

(use shorter rounder Italian rice)

1 clove garlic, crushed and chopped
1 pint beef stock (beef cube)
2 oz. butter
2 oz. mushrooms, sliced
1 can cream of tomato soup
1 large onion, finely chopped
6 oz. rice
10 oz. can luncheon meat, chopped
1 small can garden peas

Sauté the crushed chopped garlic and finely chopped onion in the butter in a pan for a few minutes. Add the rice and continue to cook until the rice becomes opaque. Pour on the stock. Stir well adding the sliced mushrooms. Cover and cook gently for some 20 minutes by which time most of the liquid will be absorbed. Add the diced luncheon meat to the rice, replace the lid and leave over low heat to warm the meat through. Check frequently that the rice is not sticking, adding a little stock if necessary. Heat the tomato soup and the peas. Drain the peas. Pile the risotto in a dish, add the peas and pour over the hot soup. Serve.

Risotto provençal

2 tablespoons olive oil
2 cups rice
1 pinch black pepper
1 glass dry white wine
2 cloves garlic, chopped
2 tablespoons parsley
½ green pepper, chopped
½ large onion, chopped
3 tomatoes, peeled and chopped
1 tablespoon finely chopped onion
1 pinch saffron

Heat oil in a saucepan and sauté onion until golden. Stir in the rice and cook until rice is golden brown. Add ¾ pint of hot water and simmer gently until water is absorbed. Place cooked rice in a covered oven-proof dish and keep warm.

The sauce
Sauté the finely chopped onion in a frying pan until translucent. Stir in the white wine and the peeled tomatoes, (tomatoes peel easily if first dipped, for seconds only, in hard-boiling water). Add the garlic, chopped parsley and powdered saffron. To powder saffron, take a few saffron threads, fold into a small piece of foil and warm in the grill pan for a few minutes. Open the foil, rub the saffron threads into an egg cup of warm water and pour into the pan. Simmer the onion, tomato and seasoning for 20 minutes. Add the chopped pepper and simmer for a further 10 minutes. Add this mixture to the cooked rice and serve.

Risotto bolognese

3 chicken livers, or 1 small tin of liver or 1 small can of kidneys
¾ pint chicken stock (chicken stock cube)
1 glass Marsala wine or sweet sherry
3 tablespoons olive oil
2 onions, chopped finely
6 oz. rice
½ teaspoon nutmeg
1 crushed chopped clove garlic
½ teaspoon marjoram
1 tablespoon chopped parsley
1 teaspoon oregano
1 bay leaf
Parmesan cheese, powdered

Cook the onions in a little oil in a pan until golden. Add the rice and stir. Slice the liver or the kidneys into thin slices and add, with the garlic, to the pan. Sauté until the rice begins to look transparent then add a glass of Marsala or Sherry. Mix all these ingredients and add the stock gradually as the rice takes up the liquid. Just before the risotto is cooked sprinkle on all the herbs, cover the pan and simmer for a few minutes. Fold in the Parmesan cheese and serve.

Pasta

All pasta is made with the same flour dough and the method of cooking is the same for most types. The Italians have over one hundred varieties of pasta. Most people would recognise three basic kinds, vermicelli, the thin 'worms', spaghetti, the medium sized tubes, and macaroni which has the thickness of a pencil. The time of cooking depends entirely upon the size of the strips. All are sold in packets of uniform length. There are, of course, a number of more exotic varieties, one shaped like small bows, another resembling little butterflies, whilst ravioli are little sachets of pasta ready stuffed with a meat filling. Whatever the shape each and every one is a vehicle for additives and accompanying sauces.

One pound of pasta is ample for 4 servings. It is cooked in plenty of well-salted water, at least 3 pints per pound. Let the water boil quickly in a large pot. When the water is bubbling introduce the pasta to the hot water without breaking. It will soften as it is immersed and can be curled around the pot. Turn down the heat and stir gently at first to prevent sticking to the pan. The time of cooking depends, of course, on the thickness of the material. Obviously the thicker varieties take longer to cook. When tender but still firm the pasta is done. Test by biting a piece. It should not be soggy or gluey but firm enough to be bitten cleanly, hence the Italian term for perfection – *al dente*. Pasta should be eaten immediately it is cooked. If it has to be kept hot for a while, drain it through a colander, place the colander over a pan of simmering water and cover with a clean cloth.

As a stop-gap meal pasta, vermicelli, spaghetti or macaroni, cooked in the above manner with baked beans and frankfurters as an additive make a warming satisfying dish. The canned pie fillings, steak and kidney, steak and onions or steak and mushrooms with some additional garlic and tomato as an additive produce Pasta Milanese.

Spaghetti quickie

8 oz. long spaghetti
1 oz. butter
Finely grated cheese to taste
10-oz. can of chopped ham
1 small can condensed tomato soup

Cook the spaghetti in plenty of boiling salted water until tender. Open a can of chopped ham and dice the meat. Fry the diced ham in a little butter until browned, shaking to prevent sticking. When spaghetti is cooked, drain thoroughly and add the rest of the butter. Add the tomato soup to the meat and heat. Pour this mixture over the spaghetti in a fire-proof dish, cover with grated cheese and brown under the grill.

Macaroni cheese

8 oz. macaroni
1 oz. butter
1 oz. flour
½ pint milk
1 small onion, sliced
1 teaspoon mixed herbs
6 black peppercorns
1½ oz. grated cheese (Cheddar)
½ teaspoon mustard
1 tablespoon tomato ketchup
Parmesan cheese

Cook the macaroni in salted water, drain, place in a shallow oven-proof dish, cover and keep warm.

Melt butter in a small pan, and when it bubbles stir in flour, a little at a time, to make a roux. Pour in the milk gradually, stirring the while. When sauce begins to thicken add the onion and herbs and continue to simmer for 15 minutes. Strain the sauce, replace on a gentle heat and add the grated cheese and mustard. Continue to stir until cheese has melted. Pour this sauce over the pasta in the dish, garnish with Parmesan cheese, dot with tomato ketchup and brown under the grill. Serve immediately.

Curry

One internationally famous yachtsman is reputed to have circled the world on curry. Such a testimonial, even if only based on folklore, cannot be dismissed. The old adage that curry was invented to disguise decomposition can be dismissed, as witness the present popularity of Indian cooking. To Indians, cooking is one of the divine arts, a god-given revelation to man, and their food preparation is approached with a reverential care and respect, a lesson all cooks could well take to heart. Curry is but one small paragraph in the cook books of the East yet it is an invaluable source of warm spicy dishes, most welcome to a cold and weary seafarer. It is said that the hotter the climate the hotter comes the curry, but there have been many times in the North Sea during a typical English summer when only the searing fires of a Deccan curry could hold the chill north-easter at bay and put heart into a semi-refrigerated crew.

Basically a curry is a stew or casserole of fish, meat, poultry, shell fish or eggs cooked in a spiced sauce. The many spices which go to make the seasoning of the dish are sold as a ground ready-made mixture, a curry powder or paste. The garam marsala, the proportions of coriander, cumin, cardamon seeds, black peppers, chillis, cinnamon bark, ginger root, laurel and turmeric are a matter of personal choice to the Indian chef en chef. The only choice the ship's cook has with the mixture is one of temperature. This is determined by the quantity of curry used in the dish. It will range from the mildly warming pinch to the 2 tablespoons of powder which may sear the taste buds, immobilise the lungs and blast the eyeballs. Season, then, carefully to taste.

Eggs vindaloo

8 hard boiled eggs
2 onions, chopped
2 tablespoons butter
1 *level* dessertspoon curry powder
1 *level* teaspoon chilli powder
1 heaped teaspoon flour
½ pint white wine vinegar
½ pint chicken stock
1 bay leaf
1 teaspoon thyme

Melt the butter in a pan and fry the curry and chilli powders for 1 minute. Blend in the flour to make a paste. Add the chopped onions and cook for 2 minutes, stirring. Add the vinegar and the stock, stirring until the mixture is smooth. Add the bay leaf, thyme and a pinch of salt, and simmer the sauce for ½ hour. Arrange the hard boiled eggs, halved lengthwise in an ovenproof dish and pour over the curry sauce, removing the bay leaf. Leave to steep for an hour in the covered dish. After an hour reheat the dish on an asbestos mat and serve immediately.

Chicken curry

2 cups canned chicken breasts, diced large (or any cooked chicken in similar fashion)
2 cups canned ham, diced large
4 tablespoons red and green chopped peppers
2 cups chicken stock (chicken stock cube)
1 + tablespoon curry powder (to taste!)
½ cup split roasted almonds
2 tablespoons butter
1 cup mushrooms, sliced
1 onion, finely chopped
2 cups single cream
½ cup grated coconut

Melt the butter in the pan and cook the onion, the peppers and the mushrooms until the onion is translucent. Stir in the stock and simmer for a few minutes, stirring. Blend the remainder of the butter, with the flour and the curry powder and stir it into the pan. Continue stirring the simmering sauce until it is smooth. Add the cream, stir in the diced chicken and ham, and continue to simmer the mixture. *Do not boil*, and stir to prevent sticking. Cook for 10 minutes. Just before serving add almonds and coconut. Serve with a salad of green vegetable and orange.

Lambrosia

2 lb of lamb stewing meat cut into cubes
¼ cup flour
1½+ teaspoons curry powder (to taste!)
3 teaspoons salt
¼ teaspoon black pepper
2 tablespoons butter
1 small carton soured cream – or single cream + lemon juice
1 cup chicken stock (chicken stock cube)

1 cup white wine
8 carrots cut in thin strips
1 can sweet corn
3 onions, sliced

Put flour, salt and pepper into a paper bag. Shake the meat in the bag and then brown it in hot oil in the open pressure cooker. Mix the flour remaining in the bag with the curry powder, stock and wine and pour into the cooker. Add the carrots and onions and bring to pressure. Cook for 35 minutes. Heat a can of sweet corn. Serve the lamb curry casserole topped with sweet corn, pour over sour cream.

Madras beef curry

2 tins stewed steak
1 large onion, chopped
2 cloves garlic, chopped
2 tablespoons cooking oil
1 tablespoon curry powder
1 cup beef stock (beef cube)
Juice ½ lemon
2 bay leaves
1 tablespoon brown sugar
2 tablespoons tomato purée

Put a little oil in a pan and fry the onion, garlic and curry powder for 3 minutes. Pour on the stock, the lemon juice and the bay leaves. Add the steak and bring to the boil. Reduce heat and add the sugar and tomato purée. Simmer for 15 minutes, stirring occasionally to prevent sticking. Remove bay leaves and serve on a bed of rice, with grated coconut, chopped apple, raisins and mango chutney on the side.

Section 20

Dessert

Or as they say in the Royal Yacht Squadron, 'pudden'.

More often than not this is the child's play section of the meals afloat programme. Since most of the meals will be eaten in a sailing season of spring and summer, fresh fruit will constitute the dessert course frequently. If fresh fruit is not to hand, there is a large range of canned fruits becoming more exotic every day, now including such tastes of far off seas and tropic islands as lichees, paw-paw and passion fruit. Fresh fruit salads with cream, canned fruit and cream or just the cream itself can be much improved with a selection of additives from the liquor locker.

Pears and bananas with a dusting of grated chocolate and a tablespoon of Tia Maria, blackberries with kirsch, pineapple with St James rum and peaches with brandy are just a few quickies with which to dismiss the dessert. One can also rapidly prepare the powdered custard, angel delight, instant whip which give the young in the crew another reason to enjoy what they are pleased to term a tuck-in, though not in the waistline.

Since the good ship's cook should be able to surprise even the most jaded of shell backs, it is a pleasant change to fry fresh fruit. Try for example fresh pineapple (or canned pineapple rings) flambéed in kirsch. If using canned fruit, drain off the juice (remember the tafra bottle). Put a knob of butter in the pan, add the fruit with some three or four spoonfuls of brown sugar. Cook until the sugar browns. Heat a tablespoon kirsch in the ladle, light, and pour over the pineapple, serve immediately, flaming. Bananas may be cooked in a similar manner with rum, and so too may peaches, with brandy.

There will be occasions when what may be termed a dessert can be served as a breakfast starter, particularly in cold weather. Grapefruit or orange, cut across and sprinkled with demerara sugar may be grilled, to be served caramelled, hot. Dried fruit mixture soaked overnight or prunes, which may be bought stoned and prepared, if boiled for just a few minutes with added sugar, the juice of a lemon and a tot of rum, make a tasty dessert or at the first meal of the day, a moving experience.

Apples and bananas are a changed dish if frittered. Make a frying batter in these proportions: 2 oz. flour to 1½ tablespoons of oil, the white of 1 egg and tepid water.

Blend the oil, flour and tepid water to give a smooth creamy consistency. Leave to stand for ½ hour. Just before using, add the white of egg beaten stiff. This will give a lighter crisp batter than if you add the egg yolk as well.

Apple fritters

Peel and core the cooking apples and cut into ¼-in. thick slices as rings. Dip into the batter and fry on both sides in hot oil. Drain the fritters on paper towels and serve dusted with castor sugar. Both bananas and pineapple rings may be cooked in the same manner.

Pancakes

Pancakes with a wide variety of sweet or savoury fillings are also a popular dessert course. The batter is a mix made from 1 oz. of flour to 1 egg to 2 tablespoons of milk. Gradually beat this mixture until smooth and bubbly. Put into the pan just sufficient oil to cover the bottom. When this is hot, pour in sufficient batter to just cover the pan. Keep shaking the pan and turn the pancake when brown on one side. Brown both sides by turning (see Frittata recipe under 'eggs'). The pancake sugared and sprinkled with nutmeg may be rolled when cooked. It can be filled with treacle, honey or jam, with clotted cream or cream cheese. Pancakes are better if not tossed in the confined space of a galley. Toss the failures – over the side.

Heavy duty puddings

There will be occasions when the frippery of fruit desserts and cream will not fit the bill. So, on those dreadful passages when the cold, cold world breathes down the neck and the dribble of icy sea water takes 15 minutes of freezing agony to run from neck to navel, the only 'pudden' to line the inner man is a good steamed duff.

The basic pudding mixture consists of:
4 oz. flour
1 teaspoon baking powder
4 oz. breadcrumbs
4 oz. margarine or chopped suet
1 egg
2 tablespoons milk
½ teaspoon salt

To this fillings will be added. The fillings may be:

1. Sultana pudding – add 2 oz. sultanas
   2 tablespoons syrup
   ½ teaspoon nutmeg
2. Date pudding – add 4 oz. chopped stoned dates
   A grated rind and juice of 1 lemon
   An extra egg
3. Ginger pudding – add 2 oz. chopped crystallised ginger
   2 teaspoons ground ginger

In every case:
Grease a pudding basin and a double sheet of greaseproof paper to cover the basin top.

Sift flour and baking powder and salt. Mix these together and rub in the margarine or stir in the suet. Add the sugar, breadcrumbs, the filling ingredients from (1) (2) or (3) and stir well. Mix the egg with the milk and if using treacle, the warmed syrup. Add the other ingredients and mix vigorously into the pudding. Fill the basin no more than $\frac{2}{3}$ full, cover with the greased paper and tie with a becket or handle to lift the basin. Put the basin into the pressure cooker, add 1 quart of water. Leave valve open and adjust heat so that steam comes gently from the open valve. Steam this for an hour for pudding to rise. Lower valve control, bring to pressure and cook for 40 minutes.

Steamed puddings are filling and warming. They should be served with a custard or treacle sauce or with jam, hot from the basin. In late autumn or winter they are staple diet for a sailing crew.

Sweet sweets

For those with a sweet tooth and particularly for the young of the family afloat whose 'oohs' and 'aahs' through smacked lips are a defiance of teething troubles to come, the following dessert delicacies are easily produced:

Raspberry ambrosia

1 can (6 oz.) cream
1 can raspberries
1 can creamed rice
1 tablespoon Cassis (blackcurrant syrup)

Mix creamed rice with cream, drain raspberries, mix with cassis and top rice with mixture. Serve.

Rich rum chocolate dessert

2 × 4 oz. packets chocolate buttons
3 teaspoons instant coffee
$\frac{3}{4}$ pint double cream (longlife)
2 tablespoons rum
2 tablespoons honey

Melt the chocolate in a bowl over boiling water in a saucepan. Dissolve instant coffee in the rum. Add melted chocolate. Whisk cream and honey until thick and stir into chocolate mix. Leave to get cold. Serve, chilled, if possible.

Party peaches

4 tablespoons red currant jelly
2 tablespoons kirsch
4 large peaches, peeled, halved and stoned (or canned peaches, drained)
Instant whip or Angel delight powder
2 tablespoons honey (clear preferably)

Melt red currant jelly and mix with cream and kirsch. Set halves of peaches in Instant whip (prepared as directed on packet). Fill peach centres with jelly, cream kirsch mix.

Section 21

FIFTY TIPS FOR THE GALLEY SLAVE

1. Buy ready-made sauces to serve with canned chicken and beef – just open up and gently heat through.

2. To save cooking space use 3 triangular saucepans on 1 burner. It saves fuel also.

3. The inserts from the pressure cooker will fit the triangular saucepans for draining purposes.

4. A stock pot will keep for several days if brought to the boil *every* day and left sealed.

5. Marinaded and turned, fresh meat will keep for several days after purchase.

6 Eggs will keep for many weeks if greased and wrapped in paper tissues.

7. Loaves are more likely to remain fresh, wrapped and sealed in foil.

8. Cook 'Take and Bake' rolls in the oven and reheat for breakfast.

9. Use plastic boxes which will fit inside each other for storing, e.g. 3 rectangular type of decreasing size rather than 1 round, 1 square, 1 rectangular.

10. Rectangular storage boxes are more economical of space than circular types.

11. When cooking potatoes include an extra one, for use with salad when cold.

12. If boiling eggs for breakfast include 1 extra for salad garnish later. Hard boil 4 extra and serve stuffed as a starter.

13. Canned mixed vegetables make a good base for a Russian salad.

14. As a change, serve grilled grapefruit for breakfast.

15. Quick desserts may be prepared in ready-made flan or meringue cases.

16. Vary salads by including fresh or tinned fruit, chopped anchovies, capers and chopped nuts.

17. Use greaseproof bags for tossing meat in seasoned flour.

18. Use canned concentrated soup as a sauce.

19. Dust fried fish with a little fennel after cooking.

20. Pickle hard boiled eggs by immersing in spiced boiling vinegar, in a preserving jar.

21. Use canned custard as an instant dessert with an added teaspoon of liqueur.

22. Foil wrap vegetables separately and cook in one pot.

23. For accompaniments to beefburgers use prepared horseradish or red currant jelly.

24. Use paper towels for mopping up and save washing the dish cloth.

25. Toasted cheese is much improved if sprinkled with a little paprika and dotted with tomato ketchup.

26. Dress up savouries and starters with small cocktail onions dyed red in beetroot juice.

27. Garnish instant dessert with glacé cherries and angelica (port and starboard).

28. Use crushed cornflakes in place of cooked breadcrumbs to top spiced dishes.

29. Canned corn and rice extend a vegetable salad when visitors suddenly arrive.

30. Stir a teaspoon of brandy into a breakfast cup of whipped cream. Use as topping for a dessert of chopped fresh fruit.

31. Serve canned asparagus tips with cold breast of chicken as a party snack.

32. A quick pasta filling can be produced from a tin of minced steak, a small tin of tomato purée and a grated onion. Pour over cooked spaghetti when heated through.

33. Any canned cream soup (chicken, asparagus, celery, mushroom) is vastly improved with 2 teaspoons of dairy cream added to each portion just before serving.

34. Grill bacon rashers until crisp. Crumble and add to a serving of baked beans or a scrambled egg.

35. Coat florets of cooked cauliflower with a concentrated cream of celery soup, top with grated cheese and brown under the grill. Makes a lunch-time quickie.

36 . Poach fillets of fish in cream of tomato soup.

37. Vary cooked rice, by cooking in canned tomato juice, serve sprinkled with chives.

38. Cook rice in chicken stock, serve sprinkled with paprika.

39. Use lentil soup as a sauce for hot dogs or frankfurters.

40. As an alternative to roasting, use an oven-proof glass casserole, with lid, on two asbestos mats over the burner.

41. Most canned prepared dishes can be cooked as a casserole on top of the stove or under the grill. A more attractive dish results.

42. At a forecast of bad weather put on a stew or soup in the pressure cooker. Leave sealed when cooked, as emergency rations.

43. Never store moist items, cheese, bacon, bread in closed polythene bags. Mildew will grow rapidly in such conditions.

44. Do not wash the frying pan. Wipe clean with paper towels whilst hot, clean with a freshly oiled towel and store.

45. Give any crew member or visitor who uses tableware as an ashtray a rocket; this includes the owner's wife. Provide ashtrays for addicts in the cockpit.

46. Wash up as you go – don't accumulate dirty dishes, for the crew may go ashore.

47. Pierce both ends of empty cans and place in the gash bag.

48. Never, never throw glass bottles overboard unless filled with sea water and sunk in the depths.

49. Never, never throw plastic gash overboard, it can stop up engine intakes.

50. TURN OFF THE GAS AT THE PRESSURISED CYLINDER AFTER USE.

Appendix A

The Galley equipment

Pots, pans and utensils

2 pressure cookers with inserts
1 3-pt. kettle (whistling type)
1 coated frying pan, with lid
3 triangular saucepans, with detachable handle
1 fish fry
1 milk saucepan
1 egg poacher
4 assorted oven-proof glass bowls, with lids
1 oven-proof glassware measuring jug
1 large (1 quart) plastic jug with lid
4 asbestos stove mats
2 kitchen aprons
2 pairs oven gloves
6 tea towels
2 plastic washing bowls
1 salad strainer (folding)
1 colander
3 kitchen knives (chopping, medium, paring)
3 vegetable peelers
1 soup ladle
1 slotted draining spoon
1 plastic slice
1 wooden stirring spoon, 1 wooden spatula
1 pr. kitchen tongs
1 pr. kitchen scissors
1 whisk
1 mincer
1 grater (folding type)
1 plastic sieve
3 tin openers, 3 bottle openers, 3 corkscrews
1 yolk separator
1 knife sharpener
1 set plastic spoon measures
1 kitchen balance (4 oz. steelyard type)
6 long skewers
12 short skewers
1 chopping board 18 in. square

Galley stores

1 large (1 gallon) detergent
1 large scouring powder
1 large (hotel size) steel scouring pads
2 dish washing brushes
6 rolls paper towels
3 boxes paper tissues
2 pkts. (100 each) cocktail sticks
2 pkts. waxed paper plates (4 dozen)
4 pkts. waxed paper cake cups (8 dozen)

Tableware and cutlery

6 large dinner plates
6 small side plates
6 soup bowls
6 dessert dishes
6 cups and saucers
6 mugs
6 egg cups
1 milk jug
1 sugar bowl
1 salt mill
1 pepper mill
6 dinner knives (steak type)
6 small knives
6 dessertspoons
6 soup spoons
12 teaspoons
2 tablespoons
2 large serving spoons

Stores containers

6 screw-topped rectangular plastic containers for bulk stores of: tea, coffee, cocoa, sugar, flour, powdered dried milk
6 rectangular plastic containers, large, for bulk stores of: soups/sauces pkts., dried vegetable pkts., pasta, rice, oil and vinegar
1 plastic bread bin
1 plastic insulated butter dish

Appendix B

General grocery bulk stores

Tea (tea bags)
Coffee (instant or ground beans)
Cocoa (tinned)
Sugar, castor and demerara
Powdered dried milk
Longlife or canned evaporated milk
Longlife or canned cream
Eggs (preserved in grease)
Butter (canned)
Margarine (4 lb plastic sealed tub)
Crispbread biscuits cases of 1 dozen pkts.
French toasts cases of 1 dozen pkts.
Biscuits for cheese in tin
Fruit cake (tinned)
Marmalade (canned)
Jams (assorted) in cans
Honey
Treacle/syrup in cans
Meat extract (jars or cubes)
Chicken and beef stock cubes
Salt/pepper/mustards
Flour
Cooking oil
Vinegar (wine, cider and malt)
Rice
Pasta (spaghetti, macaroni)
Prepared cereals (cornflakes, shredded wheat, etc.)
Porridge oats
Fruit jellies
Nuts (canned peanuts, cashew nuts, almonds, walnuts, brazil nuts)
Soups (assorted, cube types)
Sauces (assorted, pkt. types)
Custard powder
Instant dessert powder (Angel delight, Instant whip)
Cornflour
Pickles, sweet, piccalilli
Piquant sauce (Worcester)
Soy sauce
Chutney (mango, apple)
Tomato purée
Garlic cloves
Herbs in sealed containers:
(basil, bayleaves, bouquet garni, chives, dill, fennel, fines herbes, marjoram, mint, oregano, parsley, rosemary, sage, tarragon, thyme, garlic salt, celery salt, savoury)
Spices in sealed containers:
(cayenne, cloves, chillis, cinnamon, curry powder, ginger, nutmeg, paprika, saffron, turmeric)
Flavouring essences in bottles:
(lemon, orange, almond, vanilla)
Fruit Juices (orange, grapefruit, pineapple, tomato) in large cans
Snacks in packets (potato crisps, savoury biscuits)
Sandwich spreads and meat/fish pastes
Dried fruits (prunes, raisins, sultanas, dates, apricots, apple rings)

Appendix C

Preserved food stock list

Meat canned

Stewed steak
Corned beef
Beefburgers
Ham
Bacon grill
Frankfurters
Stuffed pork roll
Chicken breasts
Chicken whole
Roast pork with stuffings
Roast beef slices
Lamb casserole
Roast lamb slices
Kidneys
Tongue
Hot dogs

Fish canned

Salmon
Herrings
Tuna
Mackerel
Pilchards
Sardines
Anchovies
Cod's roe
Smoked roe
Herring roes
Kipper fillets
Mussels (jars)
Smoked Oysters
Prawns
Shrimps
Lobster tails

Vegetables canned

Peas
Cut beans
Sliced beans
Broad beans
Haricot beans
Mixed vegetables
Carrots
New potatoes
Celery
Artichoke hearts
Spinach
Sweet corn
Mushrooms
Tomatoes
Peppers

Fruit canned

Pears
Apricots
Peaches
Oranges
Pineapple
Strawberries
Cherries
Fruit salad
Olives (jars)
Beetroot (jars)
Pickled walnuts (jars)
Ratatouille (jars)

Dehydrated vegetables

Peas
Corn
Mixed vegetables
Beans

Dehydrated soups

Mushroom
Asparagus
Celery
Oxtail
Kidney
Mixed vegetable
French onion
Lentil
Minestrone

Dehydrated prepared meals

Chicken curry
Spaghetti bolognaise
Beef bourguignonne
Chilli con carne
Chow mein

Appendix D

Storage Diagram and Consumption Record

Storage Sketch Plan for 26-Foot Boat

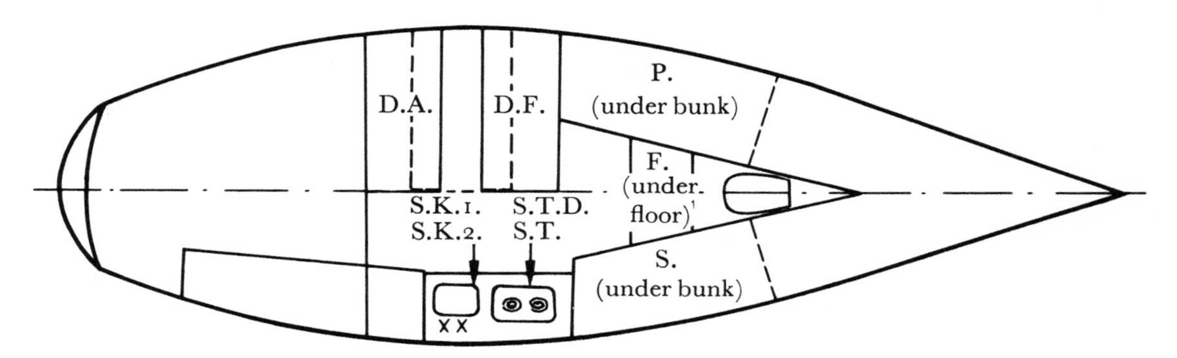

Key to Abbreviations

D.A.	Dinette Aft Locker	S.T.D.	Stove Drawers
D.F.	Dinette Forward Locker	S.T.	Stove Locker
P.	Port Locker	S.K.1.	Sink Locker 1
S.	Starboard Locker	S.K.2.	Sink Locker 2
F.	Forward Locker		

Section 1	**everyday bulk stores**		**locker stowage**
item	units		location
Instant Coffee	large tins	~~4~~ $3\frac{1}{2}$	SK 1
Tea Bags	large pkts	~~400~~ 350	SK 1
Flour	lb	~~4~~ $3\frac{1}{2}$	SK 1
Sugar	lb	14	SK 1
Oil	pints	~~16~~ 15	SK 2
Vinegar	gallons	1	SK 2

Section 2	**longer life stores**					
Milk	canned	24	23	22		DF
Butter	canned	24	23			DF
Cheese	lb	5				DF
Cereals	pkts	16	15			DA
Crispbreads	pkts	24	23			DA

Section 3	**preserved stores**					
Meat						
Beef steak	cans	36	34	42	31	D
Ham	cans	6	5			D
Pork Roll	cans	24	23			D
Bacon Grill	cans	12	11	10		P

Vegetables					
Peas	cans	24	22		S
Mushrooms	cans	12	11	10	S
Celery	cans	12	11		S

Fruit					
Pears	cans	24	22		F
Apricots	cans	12	11	10	F
Cherries	cans	12			F

Appendix E

Some European specialties of food and drink

When in Greece obtain the recipes for

cooking
Vine leaves stuffed with rice
Octopus
Squid
Kebabs

taste
Pistachio nuts
Pine kernels
Olives
Sea urchin
Fresh figs
Retsina wine

When in Italy obtain the recipes for

cooking
Caponata (lobster tails with aubergines)
Tarta pasqualina (beetroot, eggs and artichokes in pastry)
Pizza and pasta dishes

taste
Prosciutto ham
Scampi
Valpolicella (red wine)
Lacryma Christi (white wine from Vesuvius)
Strega liqueur
Punt e mes vermouth

When in Spain obtain the recipes for

cooking
Paella valenciana (saffron rice, tomato, shellfish, chicken)
Conchinillo asada (roast sucking pig)
Gazpacho (cold vegetable soup)
Huelvas à la flamenco (ham, eggs and peppers)

taste
Smoked swordfish
Spiced smoked sausages
Pomal (red wine)
Montella fino (dry white wine)
Malaga (fruity fortified wine)
Don Carlos conac
Manzanilla (dry sherry)

When in France obtain the recipes for

cooking
Cassoulet (Pork, goose and haricot beans)
Escargots (snails in garlic butter)
Tripes à la mode de Caen (tripe)

taste
Grapes
Peaches
Salsifis
Champagne
Cognac
Armagnac (brandy)

When in Brittany obtain the recipes for

cooking
Homard armoricaine (lobster in Breton fashion)
Moules marinière (mussels in brine)
Coquilles St Jacques (scallops)

taste
Fresh sardines
Fresh artichokes
Cider
Calvados (brandy)

When in the Netherlands

taste
Raw herring
Oysters (all the year round)
Turbot
Shrimps
Pastries (very rich indeed)
Aquavit
Bols, schnapps

When in Great Britain obtain the recipes for

cooking
Yorkshire pudding
Steak and kidney pudding with oyster topping
Haggis

taste
Kippered herrings
Cornish pilchards and cream
Jellied eels
Dittisham plums
Christmas pudding
Devon cider
Burton ale
Scotch whisky

Appendix F

Conversion factors

Since so many packaged foods and recipes are quoted in such a wide variety of quantities, the table below may help simple arithmetical conversion.

4 teaspoonfuls	= 1 tablespoonful
16 tablespoonfuls	= 1 cupful
1 cupful	= 10 fluid oz.
10 fluid oz.	= ½ pint
35 fluid oz.	= 1 litre
1¾ pints	= 1 litre
1 gallon	= 4.54 litres
1 oz.	= 28.3 grammes
2.2 lb	= 1 kilogramme

Conversion weights of measures for common ingredients.

1 oz. butter	= 2 tablespoonfuls
1 lb. grated cheese	= 2 cupfuls
1 oz. cocoa	= 3½ tablespoonfuls
1 oz. curry powder	= 4 tablespoonfuls
1 oz. flour	= 1 heaped tablespoonful
1 oz. jam	= 2 tablespoonfuls
1 oz. milk powder	= 3 tablespoonfuls
1 oz. porridge oats	= 4 tablespoonfuls
1 oz. dried peas	= 2 tablespoonfuls
1 oz. dehydrated potato	= 3½ tablespoonfuls
1 oz. rice	= 2 tablespoonfuls
1 oz. castor sugar	= 2 tablespoonfuls

INDEX

References to recipes are in italics.